aran & nordic knits for kids

aran & nordic knits for kids

25 designs for babies and young children

Martin Storey

photography by Steven Wooster

Aran & Nordic Knits for Kids
UK edition published in 2013 by
Rowan Yarns
Green Lane Mill
Holmfirth
West Yorkshire
HD9 2DX

Created and produced by Berry & Bridges Ltd
Belsize Business Centre
258 Belsize Road
London NW6 4BT

Designer Anne Wilson
Editor Katie Hardwicke
Styling Susan Berry
Pattern writing and knitting Penny Hill
Pattern checker Marilyn Wilson
Charts Therese Chynoweth
Illustrations Ed Berry

ISBN 978-1-907544-61-3

British Library Cataloguing and Publication Data
A catalogue record of this book is available from the
British Library

Reproduced in Singapore
Printed in China

Contents

heidi coat

A sweet, slightly flared, double-breasted coat-cum-jacket, Heidi has a lovely textured design and really great shape. It is perfect for layering over a skirt, dress, or leggings. Knitted in Rowan *Wool Cotton 4 Ply* (see pattern, page 50).

tobias hoodie

This great Aran, cabled hoodie would suit both boys and girls. It has a generous hood that extends from a shawl collar neckline. The sleeves and back are worked in plain moss stitch. Knitted in Rowan *Wool Cotton* (see pattern, page 54).

petra sweater

This lovely little sweater with its charming cat, mouse and leaf motifs, is sure to appeal to young children. The hem and cuffs are tipped in green, echoing the green leaves. A buttoned shoulder fastening makes it easy to put on and take off. Knitted in *Rowan Fine Tweed* (see pattern, page 58).

jakob cardigan

This time a button-up collared cardigan for boys features hares and foxes running around the front and back, and around the sleeves. Knitted in *Rowan Fine Tweed* (see pattern, page 62).

stefan sweater

This little boy's sweater uses one of the Nordic seafaring patterns in the form of an anchor in the centre front panel. It has a slighter lowered crew neck and a buttoned shoulder fastening. Knitted in Rowan *Wool Cotton 4 Ply* (see pattern, page 68).

lotte cardigan

These characterful little birds, interspersed with rows of simple Fairisle, make a delightful buttoned up, collared, cropped cardigan for little girls. Knitted in *Rowan Fine Tweed* (see pattern, page 72).

lotte scarf

The little bird motif (see also the Lotte cardigan) makes a great addition to a narrow scarf, knitted double, tipped with one of the colours from the bird, and with a little repeating Fairisle pattern. (The scarecrow, made by Noa who is lying next to it, looks pretty good in it too!) Knitted in *Rowan Fine Tweed* (see pattern, page 78).

sofie tunic

This sweet little tunic, with its lightly gathered skirt, sports a heart motif on the front panel. The neck is a lowered round neck, worked in moss stitch to give it a flat edge, as is the hem. Knitted in Rowan *Wool Cotton 4 Ply* (see pattern, page 80).

olle socks & mittens

Stripes are always fun to knit and a useful way of using up your 'stash' of yarns from other colourwork patterns. If you don't have quite enough of any one colour, you can ring the changes on the stripe sequence to suit. Knitted in Rowan *Felted Tweed DK* (see Socks pattern, page 84, and Mittens pattern, page 86).

alexa poncho

With its heavily cabled and bobbled front and twisted cable hem, this little poncho with a generous hood, makes a great winter cover-up but is light enough to wear as a loose sweater, too. Knitted in Rowan *Wool Cotton* (see pattern, page 88).

josef waistcoat

This little button-through waistcoat with a neat shawl collar has a great chequerboard texture pattern, which is fun to knit. Knitted in Rowan *Wool Cotton 4 Ply* (see pattern, page 92).

alphabet throw & blocks

Two more great projects that you can work on the go, as the pieces are joined later. The letters on the throw are interspersed with other simple motifs. You can use the whole alphabet, as here, or create a child's name or a simple message if you prefer. Knitted in Rowan *Felted Tweed DK* (see Throw pattern, page 96, and Blocks pattern, page 102).

morten jacket

This classic cable design with its shawl collar, makes a warm winter cover-up for a little boy. Knitted in *Rowan Fine Tweed*, it is cosy and comfortable to wear (see pattern, page 104).

mikal slipover

This little textured slipover with a split front neck, would look equally good on a little girl, perhaps in a lighter colourway. Knitted in Rowan *Wool Cotton* (see pattern, page 109).

aneka cardigan

A great classic Aran design in miniature, this makes a lovely warm cardigan for a little girl and provides the knitter with lots of interest. Knitted in Rowan *Siena 4 Ply* (see pattern, page 112).

bo cardigan

This long length cardigan is a must for all lovers of colourwork who want to make something really special for a little girl, or boy. Its brilliant 'houses' motif is worked across the fronts and the back, above a repeating border of different hearts, which also features on the sleeves. Knitted in *Rowan Fine Tweed* (see pattern, page 116).

folk scarf & bag

This great Nordic people motif features both on the pockets at each end of the striped scarf and on the matching tiny tote bag. Knitted in Rowan *Felted Tweed DK* (see Bag pattern, page 122, and Scarf pattern, page 125).

norse hat & scarf

Knitted in Rowan *Felted Tweed DK*, this simple two-tone stripe and bird's-eye Fairisle combination, with its two by two rib in a contrasting colour, is lovely to knit. It would work well for both boys and girls. (See Scarf pattern, page 127, and Hat pattern, page 129.)

lara sweater

The pattern of this charming textured sweater shows up beautifully in Rowan *Cotton Glacé*. It has a split buttoned neck to make it easy to get on and off. (See pattern, page 130.)

finn sweater

A lovely, very simple fine-cable classic sweater with a small roll neck, it has a very stretchy shape and can be worn by both boys and girls. Knitted in Rowan *Wool Cotton* (see pattern, page 134).

tundra cushion

This wonderful colourwork pattern is both classic and contemporary, and gives a touch of class to any nursery. It has a simple striped back. Knitted in Rowan *Felted Tweed DK* (see pattern, page 137).

the patterns

heidi coat

A lovely little double-breasted short coat with an A-line shape, Heidi has lots of cable and texture detail to add interest to the design. It looks equally good worn with a skirt or dress, or leggings. Rowan *Wool Cotton 4 Ply* shows up the stitch pattern beautifully but is also soft and comfortable to wear.

Sizes

To fit ages

6–9	12–18	24–36	36–48	months

Actual measurements

Chest

53	57	63	70	cm
20¾	22½	24¾	27½	in

Length to shoulder

34	38	43	49	cm
13½	15	17	19¼	in

Sleeve length

17	21	25	29	cm
6¾	8¼	9¾	11½	in

Yarn

6(6:7:7) x 50g balls of Rowan *Wool Cotton 4 Ply* Leaf 491

Needles

Pair each of 3mm (US 2/3) and 3.25mm (US 3) knitting needles
Cable needle

Extras

Stitch holders
Six buttons

Tension

28 sts and 36 rows to 10cm/4in square over rev St st using 3.25mm (US 3) needles.
36 sts and 38 rows to 10cm/4in square over cable patt using 3.25mm (US 3) needles.
Or size to obtain correct tension.

Abbreviations

K1tbl = knit through the back of the loop.

P1tbl = purl through the back of the loop.

C4B = slip next 2 sts onto a cable needle and hold at back of work, k2, then k2 from cable needle.

C4F = slip next 2 sts onto cable needle and hold at front of work, k2, then k2 from cable needle.

Cr2R = slip next st onto cable needle and hold at back of work, k1tbl, then p1 from cable needle.

Cr2L = slip next st onto cable needle and hold at front of work, p1, then k1tbl from cable needle.

See also page 141.

Note

When working from Charts, right side rows are read from right to left and wrong side rows from left to right.

Back

Using 3.25mm (US 3) needles, cast on 102(124:146:168) sts.

Row 1 (RS) P4(5:6:7), [work across row 1 of panel A, p2(4:6:8), work across row 1 of panel B, p2(4:6:8)] 5 times, work across row 1 of panel A, p4(5:6:7).

Row 2 K4(5:6:7), [work across row 2 of panel A, k2(4:6:8), work across row 2 of panel B, k2(4:6:8)] 5 times, work across row 2 of panel A, k4(5:6:7).

These 2 rows set the panels with rev St st at sides.

Work straight until back measures 16(18:21:25)cm/ 6¼(7:8¼:9¾)in from cast-on edge, ending with a wrong side row.

Dec row P4(5:6:7), * patt panel A, [p2tog] 1(2:3:4) time(s), patt panel B, [p2tog] 1(2:3:4) time(s); rep from * 4 times, then patt panel A, p4(5:6:7).

92(104:116:128) sts.

Work a further 5(6:7:8)cm/2(2¼:2¾:3¼)in, ending with a wrong side row.

Shape armholes

Cast off 3(4:5:6) sts at beg of next 2 rows.

86(96:106:116) sts.

Work straight until back measures 34(38:43:49)cm/

13½(15:17:19¼)in from cast-on edge, ending with a wrong side row.

Shape shoulders

Cast off 10(12:14:16) sts at beg of next 4 rows.

Cast off rem 46(48:50:52) sts.

Left front

Using 3.25mm (US 3) needles, cast on 40(49:58:67) sts.

Row 1 (RS) P4(5:6:7), [work across row 1 of panel A, p2(4:6:8), work across row 1 of panel B, p2(4:6:8)] twice, p2.

Row 2 K2, [k2(4:6:8), work across row 2 of panel B, k2(4:6:8), work across row 2 of panel A] twice, k4(5:6:7).

These 2 rows set the panels with rev St st at side.

Work straight until front measures 16(18:21:25)cm/ 6¼(7:8¼:9¾)in from cast-on edge, ending with a wrong side row.

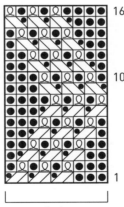

Panel A

9 sts

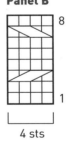

Panel B

4 sts

Key

☐	K on RS, P on WS
⊙	P on RS, K on WS
ℚ	P1tbl on WS
▨	Cr2R
◩	Cr2L
▨	C4B
▨	C4F

Dec row P4(5:6:7), * patt panel A, [p2tog] 1(2:3:4) time(s), patt panel B, [p2tog] 1(2:3:4) time(s); rep from * once, p2. *36(41:46:51) sts.*

Work a further 5(6:7:8)cm/2(2¼:2¾:3¼)in, ending with a wrong side row.

Shape armhole

Next row Cast off 3(4:5:6) sts, patt. *33(37:41:45) sts.*

Work straight until front measures 29(33:37:43)cm/ 11½(13:14½:17)in from cast-on edge, ending with a wrong side row.

Shape front neck

Next row Patt to last 2 sts, work 2tog.

Next row Work 2tog, patt to end.

Rep the last 2 rows until 20(24:28:32) sts rem.

Work straight until front measures the same as back to shoulder, ending at armhole edge.

Shape shoulder

Next row Cast off 10(12:14:16) sts, patt to end.

Work 1 row.

Cast off rem sts.

Right front

Using 3.25mm (US 3) needles, cast on 40(49:58:67) sts.

Row 1 (RS) P2, [p2(4:6:8), work across row 1 of panel B, p2(4:6:8), work across row 1 of panel A] twice, p4(5:6:7).

Row 2 K4(5:6:7), [work across row 2 of panel A, k2(4:6:8), work across row 2 of panel B, k2(4:6:8)] twice, k2.

These 2 rows set the panels with rev St st at sides.

Work straight until front measures 16(18:21:25)cm/ 6¼(7:8¼:9¾)in from cast-on edge, ending with a wrong side row.

Dec row P2, * [p2tog] 1(2:3:4) time(s), patt panel B, [p2tog] 1(2:3:4) time(s), patt panel A; rep from * once more, p4(5:6:7). *36(41:46:51) sts.*

Work a further 5(6:7:8)cm/2(2¼:2¾:3¼)in, ending with a right side row.

Shape armhole

Next row Cast off 3(4:5:6) sts, patt. 33(37:41:45) sts.

Work straight until front measures 29(33:37:43)cm/ 11½(13:14½:17)in in from cast-on edge, ending with a wrong side row.

Shape front neck

Next row Work 2tog, patt to end.

Next row Patt to last 2 sts, work 2tog.

Rep the last 2 rows until 20(24:28:32) sts rem.

Work straight until front measures the same as back to shoulder, ending at armhole edge.

Shape shoulder

Next row Cast off 10(12:14:16) sts, patt to end.

Work 1 row.

Cast off rem sts.

Sleeves

Using 3.25mm (US 3) needles, cast on 59(63:69:73) sts.

Row 1 (RS) P4(4:5:5), [work across row 1 of panel A, p4(5:6:7), work across row 1 of panel B, p4(5:6:7)] twice, work across row 1 of panel A, p4(4:5:5).

Row 2 K4(4:5:5), [work across row 2 of panel A, k4(5:6:7), work across row 2 of panel B, k4(4:6:7)] twice, work across row 2 of panel A, k4(4:5:5).

These 2 rows set the panels with rev St st at sides.

Work a further 2 rows.

Inc row P2, m1, patt to last 2 sts, m1, p2.

Work 5(7:9:11) rows.

Rep the last 6(8:10:12) rows 7 times more and the inc row again, working all inc sts into rev St st. *77(81:87:91) sts.*

Work straight until sleeve measures 17(21:25:29)cm/ 6¾(8¼:9¾:11½)in from cast-on edge, ending with a wrong side row.

Mark each end of last row with a coloured thread.

Work 2(4:6:8) rows.

Cast off.

Buttonband

Using 3.25mm (US 3) needles, cast on 39(43:47:51) sts.

Row 1 (RS) P1, [k1tbl, p1] to end.

Row 2 P1, [p1tbl, k1] to end.

These 2 rows form the twisted rib with one garter-st edge st.

Cont in rib until band fits up left front edge.

Leave these sts on a holder.

Mark position for 6 buttons, the first pair 3cm/1¼in from neck edge, the third pair level with dec row on front and the remaining pair halfway between.

Buttonhole band

Using 3.25mm (US 3) needles, cast on 39(43:47:51) sts.

Row 1 (RS) P1, [k1tbl, p1] to end.

Row 2 K1, [p1tbl, k1] to last 2 sts, p1tbl, p1.

These 2 rows form the twisted rib with one garter-st edge st.

Cont in rib until band fits up right front edge, working buttonholes to match markers as foll:

Buttonhole row (RS) Rib 4, k2tog, y2rn, skpo, rib to last 8 sts, k2tog, y2rn, skpo, rib 4.

Leave these sts on a holder.

Collar

Join shoulder seams.

With right side facing, using 3mm (US 2/3) needles, rib 37(41:45:49) sts from buttonhole band, work 2tog, pick up and k18(18:20:20) sts up right front neck edge, 45(47:49:51) from back neck, pick up and k18(18:20:20) down left side of front neck, work 2tog, rib 37(41:45:49) from buttonband. *157(167:181:191) sts.*

Cont in rib as set.

Rows 1 and 2 Rib to last 56(60:66:70) sts, turn.

Rows 3 and 4 Rib to last 53(57:62:66) sts, turn.

Rows 5 and 6 Rib to last 50(54:58:62) sts, turn.

Rows 7 and 8 Rib to last 46(50:54:58) sts, turn.

Rows 9 and 10 Rib to last 42(46:50:54) sts, turn.

Rows 11 and 12 Rib to last 38(42:46:50) sts, turn.

Change to 3.25mm (US 3) needles.

Reverse the rib from now by working k1tbl over p1 sts and p1 over k1tbl, to form fold line.

Rows 13 and 14 Rib to last 32(36:40:44) sts, turn.

Rows 15 and 16 Rib to last 26(30:34:38) sts, turn.

Rows 17 and 18 Rib to last 20(24:28:32) sts, turn.

Rows 19 and 20 Rib to last 14(18:22:26) sts, turn.

Rows 21 and 22 Rib to last 8(12:16:20) sts, turn.

Rows 23 and 24 Rib to last 4(8:10:14) sts, turn.

2nd, 3rd and 4th sizes only

Rows 25 and 26 Rib to last -(4:4:8) sts, turn.

4th size only

Rows 27 and 28 Rib to last -(-:-:4) sts, turn.

All sizes

Rib to end.

Cast off in rib.

Making up

Sew front bands in place. Join side and sleeve seams to coloured threads. Sew in sleeves. Sew on buttons.

tobias hoodie

A modern take on a traditional Aran design, this generously hooded sweater in Rowan *Wool Cotton* will have equal appeal for boys and girls. The cabled panel at the front is complimented by a plain moss stitch back and sleeves.

Sizes

To fit ages

6–9	12–18	24–36	36–48	months

Actual measurements

Chest

54	58	62	65	cm
21¼	22¾	24½	25½	in

Length to shoulder

27	30	34	39	cm
10¾	11¾	13½	15¼	in

Sleeve length

17	21	25	29	cm
6¾	8¼	9¾	11½	in

Yarn

6(7:7:8) x 50g balls of Rowan *Wool Cotton* Antique 900

Needles

Pair each of 3.75mm (US 5) and 4mm (US 6) knitting needles
3.75mm (US 5) circular needle
Cable needle

Tension

22 sts and 30 rows to 10cm/4in square over St st using 4mm (US 6) needles.
22 sts and 36 rows to 10cm/4in square over moss st using 4mm (US 6) needles.
Or size to obtain correct tension.

Abbreviations

K1tbl = knit through the back of the loop.
P1tbl = purl through the back of the loop.
C4B = slip next 2 sts onto cable needle and hold at back of work, k2, then k2 from cable needle.
C4F = slip next 2 sts onto cable needle and hold at front of work, k2, then k2 from cable needle.
C4R = slip next 2 sts onto cable needle and hold at back of work, k2, then p2 from cable needle.
C4L = slip next 2 sts onto cable needle and hold at front of work, p2, then k2 from cable needle.
T4R = slip next st onto cable needle and hold at back of work, k1tbl, p1, k1tbl, then p1 from cable needle.
T4L = slip next 3 sts onto cable needle and hold at front of work, p1, then k1tbl, p1, k1tbl, from cable needle.
T7B = slip next 4 sts onto cable needle and hold at back of work, k1tbl, p1, k1tbl, then [p1, k1tbl] twice, from cable needle.
See also page 141.

Note

When working from Charts, right side rows are read from right to left and wrong side rows from left to right.

Back

Using 3.75mm (US 5) needles, cast on 62(66:70:74) sts.
Rib row (RS) [K1, p1] to end.
Rep this row 5(7:9:11) times more.
Change to 4mm (US 6) needles.
Moss st row 1 [K1, p1] to end.
Moss st row 2 [P1, k1] to end.
These 2 rows form the moss st.
Cont in moss st until back measures14(16:19:23)cm/5½(6¼:7½:9)in from cast-on edge, ending with a wrong side row.

Shape armholes

Cast off 4 sts at beg of next 2 rows. *54(58:62:66) sts.*
Work straight until back measures 27(30:34:39)cm/ 10¾(11¾:13½:15¼)in from cast-on edge, ending with a wrong side row.

Shape shoulders

Cast off 6(7:8:9) sts at beg of next 2 rows and 7(8:9:10) sts at beg of foll 2 rows.
Cast off rem 28(28:28:28) sts.

Front

Using 3.75mm (US 5) needles, cast on 62(66:70:74) sts.
Rib row (RS) [K1, p1] to end.
Rep this row 4(6:8:10) times more.
Inc row Rib 10(12:14:16), m1, [rib 6, m1] 7 times, rib 10(12:14:16). *70(74:78:82) sts.*
Change to 4mm (US 6) needles.
Row 1 [K1, p1] 5(6:7:8) times, p2, work across row 1 of Charts A, B, A, p2, [k1, p1] 5(6:7:8) times.
Row 2 [P1, k1] 5(6:7:8) times, k2, work across row 2 of Charts A, B, A, k2, [p1, k1] 5(6:7:8) times.
These 2 rows set the cable panels with moss st at sides.
Cont in patt until front measures 14(16:19:23)cm/5½(6¼:7½:9)in from cast-on edge, ending with a wrong side row.

Shape armholes

Cast off 4 sts at beg of next 2 rows. *62(66:70:74) sts.*
Work 6 rows.

Chart A

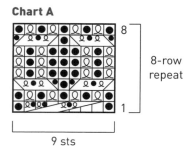

8-row repeat

9 sts

Chart B

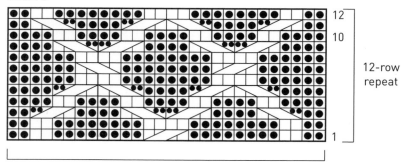

12-row repeat

28 sts

Key

☐	K on RS, P on WS
●	P on RS, K on WS
Ω	K1tbl on RS, P1tbl on WS
⟋	C4B
⟍	C4F
⟋	C4R
⟍	C4L
⟋	T4R
⟍	T4L
⟋	T7B

Divide for neck

Row 1 Patt 19(21:23:25), turn and work on these sts.

Work 3 rows.

Dec row Patt to last 14 sts, p2tog, patt to end.

Work 7 rows.

Rep the last 8 rows twice more and the dec row again. *15(17:19:21) sts.*

Work straight until front measures the same as back to shoulder, ending at armhole edge.

Shape shoulder

Next row Cast off 6(7:8:9) sts, patt to end.

Work 1 row.

Cast off rem sts.

With right side facing, rejoin yarn to rem sts, cast off centre 24 sts, patt to end. *19(21:23:25) sts.*

Work 3 rows.

Dec row Patt 12, p2tog, patt to end.

Work 7 rows.

Rep the last 8 rows twice more and the dec row again. *15(17:19:21) sts.*

Work straight until front measures the same as back to shoulder, ending at armhole edge.

Shape shoulder

Next row Cast off 6(7:8:9) sts, patt to end.

Work 1 row.

Cast off rem sts.

Sleeves

Using 3.75mm (US 5) needles, cast on 34(36:38:40) sts.

Rib row (RS) [K1, p1] to end.

Rep this row 5(7:9:11) times more.

Change to 4mm (US 6) needles.

Moss st row 1 [K1, p1] to end.

Moss st row 2 [P1, k1] to end.

These 2 rows form the moss st.

Inc and work into moss st, one st at each end of the next and every foll 4th row. *54(60:66:70) sts.*

Work straight until sleeve measures 17(21:25:29)cm/6¾(8¼:9¾:11½)in from cast-on edge, ending with a wrong side row.

Mark each end of last row with a coloured thread.

Work a further 6 rows.

Cast off.

Hood

Using 4mm (US 6) needles, cast on 42 sts.

Moss st row 1 [K1, p1] to end.

Moss st row 2 [P1, k1] to end.

These 2 rows form the moss st.

Cont in moss st until work measures 22(23:24:25)cm/8¾(9:9½:9¾)in from cast-on edge, ending with a wrong side row.

Shape top

Next row Patt 21, turn and work on these sts.

Next row Cast off 5 sts, patt to end.

Next row Patt to end.

Rep the last 2 rows twice more.

Cast off rem 6 sts.

With right side facing, rejoin yarn to rem sts.

Next row Cast off 5 sts, patt to end.

Next row Patt to end.

Rep the last 2 rows twice more.

Cast off rem sts.

Edging

Join shoulder seams. Sew cast-on edge of hood to neck edge.

With right side facing, using 3.75mm (US 5) circular needle, pick up and k30(32:34:36) sts up right side of front neck, 66(68:70:72) sts up right side of hood, 66(68:70:72) sts down left side of hood, 30(32:34:36) sts down left side of front neck. *192(200:208:216) sts.*

1st row P3, [k2, p2] to last 5 sts, k2, p3.

2nd row K3, [p2, k2] to last 5 sts, p2, k3.

Rep the last 2 rows 17 times more.

Cast off in rib.

Making up

Sew in sleeves with last 6 rows to 4 sts cast off at underarm. Join side and sleeve seams. Lap left side of hood ribbing over right and stitch in place.

petra sweater

A cute colourwork sweater that will appeal to both boys and girls, Petra is knitted in *Rowan Fine Tweed*, a yarn that really lends itself to working colour patterns. The hem, neck and cuffs are trimmed in contrasting coloured yarn. The side buttons at the neck make getting it on and off much easier!

Sizes

To fit ages

| 6–9 | 12–18 | 24–36 | 36–48 | months |

Actual measurements

Chest

| 54 | 59 | 64 | 68 | cm |
| 21¼ | 23¼ | 25 | 26¾ | in |

Length to shoulder

| 29 | 32 | 36 | 41 | cm |
| 11½ | 12½ | 14¼ | 16¼ | in |

Sleeve length

| 17 | 21 | 25 | 29 | cm |
| 6¾ | 8¼ | 9¾ | 11½ | in |

Yarns

Rowan Fine Tweed

4(5:5:6) x 25g balls Arncliffe 360 (M)

One ball each Nidd 382 (A), Settle 374 (B), Richmond 381 (C) and Hawes 362 (D)

Needles

Pair each of 2.75mm (US 2) and 3.25mm (US 3) knitting needles

Extras

Stitch holders

3 buttons

Tension

26 sts and 36 rows to 10cm/4in square over patt on 3.25mm (US 3) needles, *or size to obtain correct tension.*

Abbreviations

See page 141.

Note

When working from Chart, right side rows are read from right to left and wrong side rows from left to right. Use the Fairisle method and strand yarn across back of work over no more than 3 sts. For the size you are making, take off the centre st from the number of sts you have left, divide the remainder by 2 and count this number either side of the centre st, this will be your starting and finishing point.

Back

Using 2.75mm (US 2) needles and C, cast on 73(79:85:91) sts.

Rib row 1 K1, [p1, k1] to end.

Break off C.

Cont in M.

Rib row 2 P1, [k1, p1] to end.

Rep the last 2 rib rows 5(6:6:7) times more.

Change to 3.25mm (US 3) needles.

Work in St st and patt from Chart.

When chart is completed, cont in M only until back measures 28(31:35:40)cm/11(12¼:13¾:15¾)in from cast-on edge, ending with a purl row.

Shape upper arms

Cast off 4 sts at beg of next 2 rows and 4(5:6:7) sts at beg of foll 2 rows. *57(61:65:69) sts.*

Cast off 14(15:16:17) sts, knit to last 14(15:16:17) sts, p0(1:0:1), [k1, p1] 7(7:8:8) times, turn and work in rib on these 14(15:16:17) sts.

Work a further 6 rows.

Cast off in rib.

Leave rem 29(31:33:35) sts on a holder.

Front

Work as given for back until front measures 24(26:30:34)cm/9½(10¼:11¾:13½)in from cast-on edge, ending with a wrong side row.

Shape front neck

Next row K27(29:31:33) sts, turn and work on these sts for first side of neck shaping.

Dec one st at neck edge on the next 5 rows. *22(24:26:28) sts.*

Work straight until 4 rows less have been worked than on back to upper arm shaping, ending with a purl row.

Next row K8(9:10:11), [p1, k1] 7(7:8:8) times, p0(1:0:1).

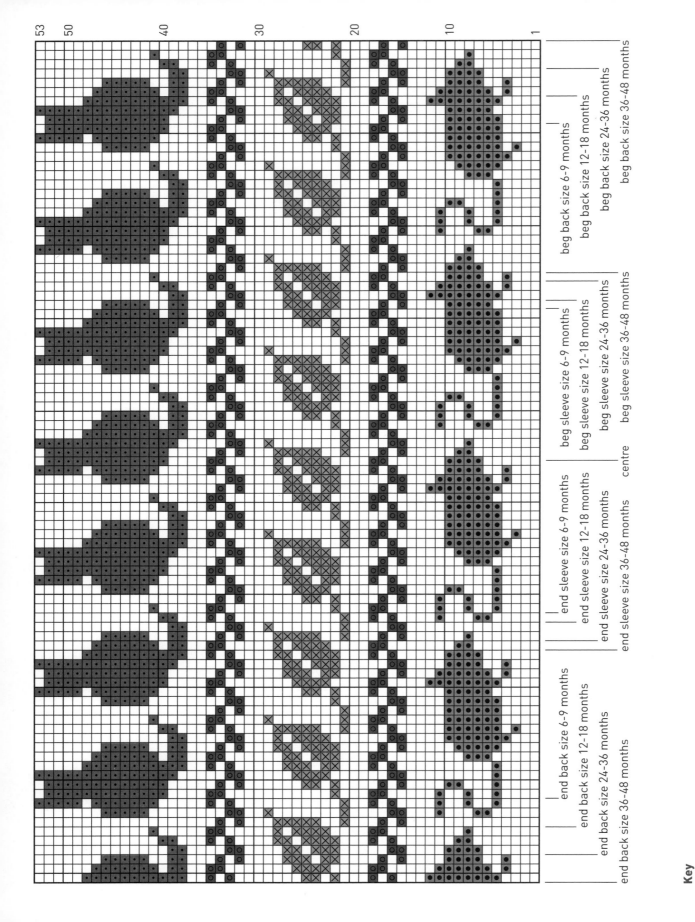

Key

- ☐ Arncliffe (M)
- ⊡ Settle (B)
- ▣ Hawes (D)
- ▣ Nidd (A)
- ☒ Richmond (C)

Next row Rib 14(15:16:17), p8(9:10:11).
Buttonhole row K8(9:10:11), rib 3, yf, k2tog, rib 5, yrn, p2tog, rib to end.
Work 1 row.

Shape upper arm
Cast off 4 sts at beg of next row and 4(5:6:7) sts at beg of foll right side row.
Cast off in rib.
With right side facing, slip centre 19(21:23:25) sts on a holder, rejoin yarn to rem sts, knit to end.
Dec one st at neck edge on the next 5 rows.
22(24:26:28) sts.
Work straight until front measures the same as upper arm shaping, ending at side edge.

Shape upper arm
Cast off 4 sts at beg of next row and 4(5:6:7) sts at beg of foll wrong side row.
Work 1 row.
Cast off.

Sleeves
Using 2.75mm (US 2) needles and C, cast on 32(34:38:40) sts.
Next row [K1, p1] to end.
This row forms the rib.
Break off C.
Join on M.
The last row forms the rib.
Work 11(13:13:15) more rows, inc one st at end of last row. *33(35:39:41) sts.*
Change to 3.25mm (US 3) needles. Work in St st and patt from Chart.
Inc and work into patt one st at each end of the 5th and every foll 4th row until there are 57(61:65:71) sts.
Cont straight until sleeve measures 17(21:25:29)cm/ 6¾(8¼:9¾:11½)in from cast-on edge, ending with a wrong side row.
Cast off.

Neckband
Join right shoulder seam.
With right side facing, using 2.75mm (US 2) needles and M, pick up and k15(17:17:19) sts down left side of front neck, k19(21:23:25) sts from front neck holder, pick up and k15(17:17:19) sts up right side of front neck, k29(31:33:35) sts from back neck holder, pick up and k7 sts along row ends of buttonband.
85(93:97:105) sts.
Rib row 1 K1, [p1, k1] to end.
Rib row 2 P1, [k1, p1] to end.
Buttonhole row Rib to last 5 sts, yrn, p2tog, rib 3.
Rib 2 more rows.
Break off M.
Join on B.
Rib 2 more rows.
Cast off in rib.

Making up
Lap buttonhole band over buttonband and stitch in place. Sew on sleeves. Join side and sleeve seams. Sew on buttons.

jakob cardigan

A cardigan this time, with another lovely colourwork design, also knitted in *Rowan Fine Tweed*. In Jakob, the pattern goes around the sleeves as well as across the fronts and back.

Sizes

To fit ages

| 6–9 | 12–18 | 24–36 | 36–48 | months |

Actual measurements

Chest

| 54 | 58 | 62 | 66 | cm |
| 21¼ | 22¾ | 24½ | 26 | in |

Length to shoulder

| 29 | 32 | 36 | 41 | cm |
| 11½ | 12½ | 14¼ | 16¼ | in |

Sleeve length

| 17 | 21 | 25 | 29 | cm |
| 6¾ | 8¼ | 9¾ | 11½ | in |

Yarns

Rowan Fine Tweed

5(5:6:6) x 25g balls Nappa 380 (M)
One ball each Pendle 377 (A), Malham 366 (B),
Hubberholme 370 (C) and Dent 373 (D)

Needles

Pair each of 2.75mm (US 2) and 3.25mm (US 3) knitting
needles

Extras

Stitch holders
5(5:6:6) buttons

Tension

26 sts and 36 rows to 10cm/4in square over patt on
3.25mm (US 3) needles, *or size to obtain correct tension*.

Abbreviations

See page 141.

Note

When working from Charts, right side rows are read
from right to left and wrong side rows from left to
right.

Back

Using 2.75mm (US 2) needles and M, cast on
73(79:85:91) sts.

Rib row 1 K1, [p1, k1] to end.

Rib row 2 P1, [k1, p1] to end.

Rep the last 2 rows 5(6:6:7) times more.

Change to 3.25mm (US 3) needles.

Work in St st and patt from Charts.

Row 1 Using M, knit to end.

Row 2 Using M, purl to end.

Row 3 K3(5:7:9)M, [knit across 21 sts of row 1 of rabbit
motif, k2(3:4:5)M] twice, work across row 1 of rabbit
motif, k3(5:7:9)M.

Row 4 P3(5:7:9)M, [purl across 21 sts of row 2 of rabbit
motif, p2(3:4:5)M] twice, work across row 2 of rabbit
motif, p3(5:7:9)M.

These 2 rows set the patt.

Work a further 13 rows to complete motif.

Rows 18 and 19 Work 2 rows M.

Row 20 Using B, purl to end.

Row 21 K1B, [5M, 1B] to end.

Row 22 P1B, [1M, 3B, 1M, 1B] to end.

Row 23 As row 21.

Row 24 As row 20.

Rows 25 and 26 Work 2 rows M.

Row 27 K2(3:4:5)M, [knit across 14 sts of row 1 of leaf
motif, k0(1:2:3)M] 4 time(s), work across row 1 of leaf
motif, k1(2:3:4)M.

Row 28 P1(2:3:4)M, [purl across 14 sts of row 2 of leaf
motif, p0(1:2:3)M] 4 time(s), work across row 2 of leaf
motif, p2(3:4:5)M.

These 2 rows set the patt.

Work a further 7 rows to complete motif.

Rows 36–44 As rows 18–26.

Row 45 K8(9:4:4)M, [knit across 18 sts of row 1 of fox
motif, k2(4:2:4)M] 2(2:3:3) times, work across row 1 of
fox motif, k7(8:3:3)M.

Row 46 P7(8:3:3)M, [purl across 18 sts of row 2 of fox
motif, p2(4:2:4)M] 2(2:3:3) times, work across row 2 of
fox motif, p8(9:4:4)M.

Fox Motif

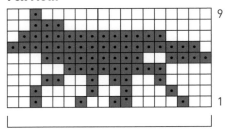

18-st repeat

Leaf Motif

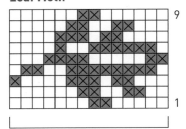

14-st repeat

Rabbit Motif

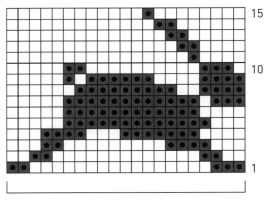

21-st repeat

Key

☐ Nappa (M)

⬤ Pendle (A)

☒ Hubberholme (C)

▣ Dent (D)

These 2 rows set the patt.

Work a further 7 rows to complete motif.

Rows 54–60 As rows 18–24.

1st and 2nd sizes only

Work rows 1–24 again.

3rd and 4th sizes only

Work rows 1–42 again.

All sizes

Cont in M only until back measures 28(31:35:40)cm/ 11(12¼:13¾:15¾)in from cast-on edge, ending with a purl row.

Shape upper arms

Cast off 4 sts at beg of next 2 rows and 4(5:6:7) sts at beg of foll 2 rows. *57(61:65:69) sts.*

Cast off 7(7:8:8) sts at beg of next 2 rows and 7(8:8:9) sts at beg of foll 2 rows.

Cast off rem 29(31:33:35) sts.

Left front

Using 2.75mm (US 2) needles and M, cast on 41(43:47:49) sts.

Rib row 1 P1, [k1, p1] to last 2 sts, k2.

Rib row 2 K1, [p1, k1] to end.

Rep the last 2 rows twice more.

Buttonhole row Rib to last 8 sts, p2tog, y2rn, k2tog, rib 4.

Work a further 4(6:6:8) rows.

Next row Rib 11, leave these sts on a holder, cast on one st, rib to end, inc 1(2:1:2) st(s) evenly. *32(35:38:41) sts.*

Change to 3.25mm (US 3) needles.

Work in St st and patt from Charts.

Row 1 Using M, knit to end.

Row 2 Using M, purl to end.

Row 3 K3(5:7:9)M, knit across 21 sts of row 1 of rabbit motif, k2(3:4:5)M, knit across first 6 sts of row 1 of rabbit motif.

Row 4 Purl across last 6 sts of row 2 of rabbit motif, p2(3:4:5)M, work across row 2 of rabbit motif, p3(5:7:9)M.

Work a further 13 rows to complete motif.

Rows 18 and 19 Work 2 rows M.

Row 20 Using B, purl to end.

Row 21 K1B, [5M, 1B] to last 1(4:1:4) st(s), 1(4:1:4)M.

Row 22 P0(3:0:3)B, 0(1:0:1)M, 2(1:2:1)B, [1M, 3B, 1M, 1B] to end.

Row 23 As row 21.

Row 24 As row 20.

Rows 25 and 26 Work 2 rows M.

Row 27 K2(3:4:5)M, knit across 14 sts of row 1 of leaf motif, k0(1:2:3)M across row 1 of leaf motif, k2(3:4:5)M.

Row 28 P2(3:4:5)M, purl across 14 sts of row 2 of leaf motif, p0(1:2:3)M, purl across row 2 of leaf motif, p2(3:4:5)M.

These 2 rows set the patt.

Work a further 7 rows to complete motif.

Rows 36–44 As rows 18–26.

Row 45 K3(5:7:9)M, knit across 18 sts of row 1 of fox motif, k2(3:4:5), knit across first 9 sts of row 1 of fox motif.

Row 46 Purl across last 9 sts of row 2 of fox motif, p2(3:4:5)M, purl across row 2 of fox motif, p3(5:7:9)M.

These 2 rows set the patt.

Work a further 7 rows to complete motif.

Rows 54–60 As rows 18–24.

These 60 rows set the patt.

Work rows 1–24(24:42:42) again and then cont in M only, **at the same time** when front measures 24(26:30:34)cm/9½(10¼:11¾:13½)in from cast-on edge, ending with a wrong side row.

Shape front neck

Next row Patt to last 5(6:7:8) sts, turn and leave these sts on a holder.

Dec one st at neck edge on every right side row until 22(24:26:28) sts rem.

Work straight until front measures the same as back to upper arm shaping, ending at side edge.

Shape upper arm

Cast off 4 sts at beg of next row and 4(5:6:7) sts at beg of foll right side row. *14(15:16:17) sts.*

Work 1 row.

Shape shoulder

Cast off 7(7:8:8) sts at beg of next row.

Work 1 row.

Cast off rem sts.

Right front

Using 2.75mm (US 2) needles and M, cast on 41(43:47:49) sts.

Rib row 1 K2, p1, [k1, p1] to end.

Rib row 2 K1, [p1, k1] to end.

Rep the last 2 rows 4(5:5:6) times more and the first row again.

Next row Inc 1(2:1:2) st(s) evenly rib to last 11 sts, leave these sts on a holder, cast on one st.
32(35:38:41) sts.

Change to 3.25mm (US 3) needles.

Work in St st and patt from Charts.

Row 1 Using M, knit to end.

Row 2 Using M, purl to end.

Row 3 Knit across last 6 sts of row 1 of rabbit motif, k2(3:4:5)M, knit across 21 sts of row 1 of rabbit motif, k3(5:7:9)M.

Row 4 P3(5:7:9)M, purl across row 2 of rabbit motif, p2(3:4:5)M, purl across first 6 sts of row 2 of rabbit motif.

Work a further 13 rows to complete motif.

Rows 18 and 19 Work 2 rows M.

Row 20 Using B, purl to end.

Row 21 K1(4:1:4)M, 1B, [5M, 1B] to end.

Row 22 P[1B, 1M, 3B, 1M] to last 2(5:2:5) sts, 2(1:2:1)B, 0(1:0:1)M, 0(3:0:3)B.

Row 23 As row 21.

Row 24 As row 20.

Rows 25 and 26 Work 2 rows M.

Row 27 K2(3:4:5)M, knit across 14 sts of row 1 of leaf motif, k0(1:2:3)M, knit across row 1 of leaf motif, k2(3:4:5)M.

Row 28 P2(3:4:5)M, purl across 14 sts of row 2 of leaf motif, p0(1:2:3)M, work across row 2 of leaf motif, p2(3:4:5)M.

These 2 rows set the patt.

Work a further 7 rows to complete motif.

Rows 36–44 As rows 18–26.

Row 45 Knit across last 9 sts of row 1 of fox motif, k2(3:4:5)M, knit across 18 sts of row 1 of fox motif, k3(5:7:9)M.

Row 46 P3(5:7:9)M, purl across 18 sts of row 2 of fox motif, p2(3:4:5)M, purl across first 9 sts of row 2 of fox motif.

These 2 rows set the patt.

Work a further 7 rows to complete motif.

Rows 54–60 As rows 18–24.

These 60 rows set the patt.

Work rows 1–24(24:42:42) again and then cont in M only, **at the same time** when front measures 24(26:30:34)cm/9½(10¼:11¾:13½)in from cast-on edge, ending with a wrong side row.

Shape front neck

Next row Patt 5(6:7:8) sts, leave these sts on a holder, patt to end.

Dec one st at neck edge on every right side row until 22(24:26:28) sts rem.

Work straight until front measures the same as back to upper arm shaping, ending at side edge.

Shape upper arm

Cast off 4 sts at beg of next row and 4(5:6:7) sts at beg of foll wrong side row. *14(15:16:17) sts.*

Work 1 row.

Shape shoulder

Cast off 7(7:8:8) sts at beg of next row.

Work 1 row.

Cast off rem sts.

Sleeves

Using 2.75mm (US 2) needles and M, cast on 32(34:38:40) sts.

Next row [K1, p1] to end.

This row forms the rib.

Work 11(13:13:15) more rows, inc one st at end of last row. *33(35:39:41) sts.*

Change to 3.25mm (US 3) needles.

Row 1 Using M, knit to end.

Row 2 Using M, purl to end.

Row 3 K6(7:9:10)M, knit across 21 sts of row 1 of rabbit motif, k6(7:9:10)M.

Row 4 P6(7:9:10)M, purl across 21 sts of row 2 of rabbit motif, p6(7:9:10)M.

These 2 rows set the patt.

Work a further 13 rows to complete motif, at the same time, inc one st at each end of the next and 3 foll 4th rows. *41(43:47:49) sts.*

Rows 18 and 19 Work 2 rows M.

Row 20 Using B, purl to end, inc one st at each end. *43(45:49:51) sts.*

Row 21 K0(1:3:4)M, 1B, [5M, 1B] to last 0(1:3:4) st(s), k0(1:3:4)M.

Row 22 P0(0:2:3)B, 0(1:1:1)M, 1B, [1M, 3B, 1M, 1B] to last 4(5:7:4) sts, 0(1:1:1)M, 0(0:2:3)B.

Row 23 As row 21.

Row 24 As row 20. *45(47:51:53) sts.*

Rows 25 and 26 Work 2 rows M.

Row 27 K2(2:3:3)M, [knit across 14 sts of row 1 of leaf motif, k0(1:2:3)M] twice, work across row 1 of leaf motif, k1(1:2:2)M.

Row 28 P1(1:2:2)M, [purl across 14 sts of row 2 of leaf motif, p0(1:2:3)M] twice, work across row 2 of leaf motif, p2(2:3:3)M.

These 2 rows set the patt.

Work a further 7 rows to complete motif **at the same time,** inc one st at each end of next and foll 4th row. *49(51:55:57) sts.*

Rows 36 and 37 Work 2 rows M.

Row 38 Using B, purl to end, inc one st at each end. *51(53:57:59) sts.*

Row 39 K4(5:1:2)M, 1B, [5M, 1B] to last 4(5:1:2) st(s), k4(5:1:2)M.

Row 40 P0(1:0:0)M, 3(3:0:1)B, 1M, 1B, [1M, 3B, 1M, 1B] to last 4(5:1:2) sts, 1M, 3(3:0:1)B, 0(1:0:0)M.

Row 41 As row 39.

Row 42 As row 38. *53(55:59:61) sts.*

Rows 43 and 44 Work 2 rows M.

1st and 2nd sizes only

Cont in M only, inc one st at each end of the next and 1(2) foll 4th rows. *57(61) sts.*

Cont straight until sleeve measures 17(21:-:-)cm/ 6¾(8¼:-:-)in from cast-on edge, ending with a wrong side row.

Cast off.

3rd and 4th sizes only

Row 45 K-(-:10:11)M, knit across 18 sts of row 1 of fox motif, k-(-:2:4)M, work across row 1 of fox motif, k-(-:11:10)M.

Row 46 P-(-:11:10)M, purl across 18 sts of row 2 of fox motif, p-(-:2:4)M, work across row 2 of fox motif, p-(-:10:11)M.

These 2 rows set the patt.

Work a further 7 rows to complete motif **at the same time,** inc one st at each end of next and foll 4th row. *-(-:63:65) sts.*

Cont in M only, inc one st at each end of the next and –(-:1:2) foll 4th rows. *-(-:67:71) sts.*

Cont straight until sleeve measures -(-:25:29)cm/ -(-:9¾:11½)in from cast-on edge, ending with a wrong side row.

Cast off.

Buttonband

With wrong side facing, using 2.75mm (US 2) needles and M, cast on one st, rib across sts on right front. *12 sts.*

Work in rib until band fits up right front to beg of neck shaping, ending with a right side row.

Leave these sts on a holder.

Mark position for 5(5:6:6) buttons, the first in 7th row of rib, the last 2 rows below neck shaping.

Buttonhole band

With right side facing, using 2.75mm (US 2) needles and M, cast on one st, rib across sts on left front. *12 sts.*

Work in rib until band fits up left front to beg of neck shaping, ending with a wrong side row and working buttonholes to match markers.

Buttonhole row Rib to last 4 sts, p2tog, y2rn, k2tog, rib 4.

Leave these sts on a holder.

Collar

Join shoulder seams.

With right side facing, using 2.75mm (US 2) needles and M, slip sts from right front band onto a needle, then slip 5(6:7:8) sts from right front onto same holder, pick up and k16(18:20:22) sts up right side of neck, cast on 45(47:51:53) sts, pick up and k16(18:20:22) sts down left side of front neck, k5(6:7:8) sts from left front, the rib 12 sts from buttonhole band. *111(119:129:137) sts.*

Cont in rib as set.

Next 2 rows Rib to last 33(36:39:42) sts, turn.

Next 2 rows Rib to last 29(32:35:38) sts, turn.

Next 2 rows Rib to last 25(28:31:34) sts, turn.

Next 2 rows Rib to last 21(23:25:27) sts, turn.

Next 2 rows Rib to last 17(18:19:20) sts, turn.

Next 2 rows Rib to last 13(13:13:13) sts, turn.

Next row Rib to end.

Work 2 rows across all sts.

Cast off 8 sts at beg of next 2 rows.

Work a further 16(18:20:22) rows. *95(103:113:121) sts.*

Cast off in rib.

Making up

Sew cast-on edge of collar to cast-off sts at back neck. Sew bands in place. Sew on sleeves, placing centre of cast-off edge to shoulder seam. Join side and sleeve seams. Sew on buttons.

stefan sweater

A simple but effective anchor design as a front panel creates a cute Guernsey-style sweater for boys or girls. Knitted in Rowan *Wool Cotton 4 Ply*.

Sizes

To fit ages

6–9	12–18	24–36	36–48	months

Actual measurements

Chest

55	59	63	68	cm
21½	23¼	24¾	26¾	in

Length to shoulder

27	30	34	39	cm
10½	11¾	13½	15½	in

Sleeve length

17	21	25	29	cm
6¾	8¼	9¾	11½	in

Yarn

3(3:4:4) x 50g balls of Rowan *Wool Cotton 4 Ply*
Paper 486

Needles

Pair each of 2.75mm (US 2) and 3.25mm (US 3) knitting needles
Cable needle

Extras

Stitch holders
2 buttons

Tension

28 sts and 36 rows to 10cm/4in square over St st on 3.25mm (US 3) needles, *or size to obtain correct tension.*

Abbreviations

BC = slip next st onto cable needle and hold at back of work, k1, then p1 from cable needle.

FC = slip next st onto cable needle and hold at front of work, p1, then k1 from cable needle.

C2F = slip next st onto cable needle and hold at front of work, k1, then k1 from cable needle.

Cr2 = skip the first st, then purl the 2nd st, then purl the skipped st and slip both sts from the needle together.

Cr3B = slip next 2 sts onto cable needle and hold at back of work, k1, then k2 from cable needle.

Cr3F = slip next st onto cable needle and hold at front of work, k2, then k1 from cable needle.

C4B = slip next 2 sts onto cable needle and hold at back of work, k2, then k2 from cable needle.

MB = make bobble, [k1, p1, k1] all in next st, turn, p3, turn, sl 1, k2tog, psso.

See also page 141.

Note

When working from Chart, right side rows are read from right to left and wrong side rows from left to right.

Back

Using 2.75mm (US 2) needles, cast on 79(85:91:97) sts.

Rib row 1 K1, [p1, k1] to end.

Rib row 2 P1, [k1, p1] to end.

Rep the last 2 rows 5(6:6:7) times more.

Change to 3.25mm (US 3) needles.

Beg with a knit row, work in St st until back measures 16(18:21:25)cm/6¼(7:8¼:9¾)in from cast-on edge, ending with a wrong side row.

Shape armholes

Cast off 4(4:5:5) sts at beg of next 2 rows.

71(77:81:87) sts.

Next row K1, skpo, knit to last 3 sts, k2tog, k1.

Next row Purl to end.

Rep the last 2 rows 3(4:4:5) times more.

63(67:71:75) sts.

Work straight until back measures 27(30:34:39)cm/10½(11¾:13½:15¼)in from cast-on edge, ending with a wrong side row.

Shape shoulders

Rows 1 and 2 Cast off 7(8:8:9) sts, knit to last 7(8:8:9) sts, turn, purl to end.

Row 3 Cast off 8(8:9:9) sts, knit to last 15(16:17:18) sts, [k1, p1] 7(8:8:9) times, k1(0:1:0).

Rows 4 and 5 P1(0:1:0), [k1, p1] 7(8:8:9) times, turn, [k1, p1] 7(8:8:9) times, k1(0:1:0).

Rep the last 2 rows once more.

Cast off in rib.

Leave centre 33(35:37:39) sts on a holder.

Front

Work straight until front measures 7(9:12:16)cm/2¾(3½:4¾:6¼)in from cast-on edge, ending with a wrong side row, inc one st at centre of last row.

80(86:92:98) sts.

Place anchor motif

Row 1 K23(26:29:32), work across row 1 of motif, k23(26:29:32).

Row 2 P23(26:29:32), work across row 2 of motif, p23(26:29:32).

These 2 rows set the motif position.

Working correct patt rows, cont straight until front measures 16(18:21:25)cm/6¼(7:8¼:9¾)in from cast-on edge, ending with a wrong side row.

Shape armholes

Cast off 4(4:5:5) sts at beg of next 2 rows.

72(78:82:88) sts.

Next row K1, skpo, knit to last 3 sts, k2tog, k1.

Next row Purl to end.

Rep the last 2 rows 3(4:4:5) times more.

64(68:72:76) sts.

Cont in patt to end of chart.

Dec one st at centre of next row, work straight until front measures 23(26:29:34)cm/9(10¼:11½:13½)in from cast-on edge, ending with a wrong side row.

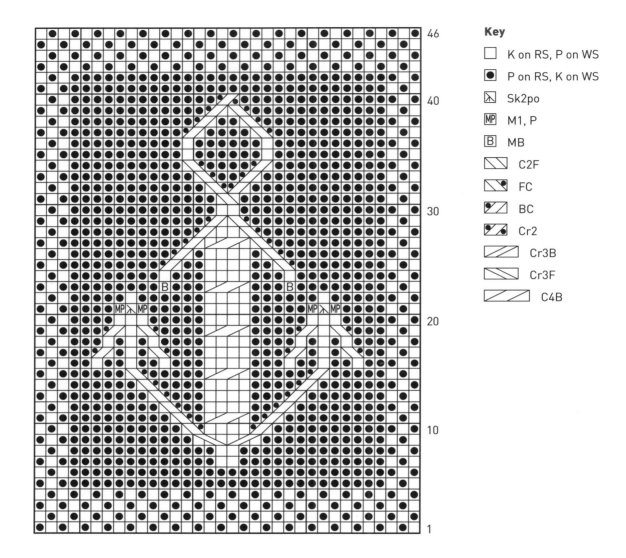

Key

☐	K on RS, P on WS
⬤	P on RS, K on WS
◩	Sk2po
MP	M1, P
B	MB
◻	C2F
◻	FC
◻	BC
◻	Cr2
◻	Cr3B
◻	Cr3F
◻	C4B

Shape front neck

Row 1 K20(21:22:23), turn and work on these sts for first side on neck shaping.

Row 2 P2tog, purl to end.

Row 3 Knit to last 2 sts, k2tog.

Rep the last 2 rows once more and row 2 again. *15(16:17:18) sts.*

Work straight until 5 rows less have been worked than on back to shoulder.

Shape shoulder

Rows 1 and 2 P7(8:8:9), turn, knit to end.

Buttonhole band

Row 3 [K1, p1] 7(8:8:9) times, k1(0:1:0).

Row 4 P1(0:1:0), [k1, p1] 7(8:8:9) times.

Rep the last 2 rows once more.

Buttonhole row Rib to last 5(6:7:8) sts, yrn, p2tog, rib 3(4:5:6).

Work 2 rows.

Cast off in rib.

With right side facing, slip centre 24(26:28:30) sts on a holder, rejoin yarn to rem sts, patt to end.

Row 2 Purl to last 2 sts, p2tog tbl.

Row 3 Skpo, knit to end.

Rep the last 2 rows once more and row 2 again. *15(16:17:18) sts.*

Work straight until front measures the same as back to shoulder, ending at armhole edge.

Shape shoulder

Next row Cast off 7(8:8:9) sts, purl to end.

Work 1 row.

Cast off rem sts.

Sleeves

Using 2.75mm (US 2) needles, cast on 34(36:38:40) sts.

Next row [K1, p1] to end.

This row forms the rib.

Work 9(11:13:15) more rows.

Change to 3.25mm (US 3) needles.

Beg with a knit row, cont in St st.

Work 2 rows.

Inc row K3, m1, knit to last 3 sts, m1, k3.

Work 3 rows.

Rep the last 4 rows 10(11:14:15) times more and the inc row again. *58(62:70:74) sts.*

Cont straight until sleeve measures 17(21:25:29)cm/ 6¾(8¼:9¾:11½)in from cast-on edge, ending with a wrong side row.

Shape top

Cast off 4(4:5:5) sts at beg of next 2 rows. *50(54:60:64) sts.*

Next row K1, skpo, knit to last 3 sts, k2tog, k1.

Next row Purl to end.

Rep the last 2 rows 3(3:4:4) times more. *42(46:50:54) sts.*

Cast off.

Neckband

Join right shoulder seam.

With right side facing, 2.75mm (US 2) needles, pick up and k16(16:18:18) sts down left side of front neck, k24(26:28:30) sts from front neck holder, dec one st at centre, pick up and k16(16:18:18) sts up right side of front neck, k33(35:37:39) sts from back neck, then pick up and k5 sts along buttonband. *93(97:105:109) sts.*

Rib row 1 K2, [p1, k1] to last 3 sts, p1, k2.

Rib row 2 K1, [p1, k1] to end.

Buttonhole row K2, p1, s2kpo, rib to last 5 sts, p2tog, yrn, p1, k2.

Rib 2 rows.

Cast off in rib.

Making up

Sew on sleeves. Join side and sleeve seams. Sew on buttons.

lotte cardigan

Cute birds parade around this cropped, box-shaped cardigan, interspersed with traditional Nordic snowflake motifs. The shawl collar, hem and cuffs are knitted in moss stitch. Knitted in *Rowan Fine Tweed*.

Sizes

To fit ages

| 6–9 | 12–18 | 24–36 | 36–48 | months |

Actual measurements

Chest

| 55 | 59 | 63 | 67 | cm |
| 21½ | 23¼ | 24¾ | 26¼ | in |

Length to shoulder

| 22 | 25 | 29 | 34 | cm |
| 8¾ | 10 | 11½ | 13½ | in |

Sleeve length

| 17 | 21 | 25 | 29 | cm |
| 6¾ | 8¼ | 9¾ | 11½ | in |

Yarns

Rowan Fine Tweed

5(5:6:6) x 25g balls Buckden 364 (M)

One ball each Askrigg 365 (A), Skipton 379 (B) and Richmond 381 (C)

Needles

Pair each of 3mm (US 2/3) and 3.25mm (US 3) knitting needles

Circular 3mm (US 2/3) and 3.25mm (US 3) needle

Extras

4(4:5:6) buttons

Tension

28 sts and 34 rows to 10cm/4in square over patt using 3.25mm (US 3) needles, *or size to obtain correct tension.*

Abbreviations

See page 141.

Note

When working from Charts, right side rows are read from right to left and wrong side rows from left to right. Use the Fairisle method, strand the yarn not in use across the wrong side of work, weaving them under and over the working yarn every 3 or 4 sts.

Back and Fronts

(worked in one piece to armholes)

Using 3mm (US 2/3) circular needle and M, cast on 165(191:191:207) sts.

Moss st row (RS) K1, [p1, k1] to end.

This row forms the moss st.

Work a further 5(7:9:11) rows.

Change to 3.25mm (US 3) circular needle.

Beg with a knit row, work in St st.

Work 2 rows.

Work rows 1–8 from Chart 1.

Using M, work 2(4:6:8) rows, inc(dec:dec:inc) 1(1:1:7) st(s) evenly across last row. *166(190:190:214) sts.*

Work in patt from Chart 2.

Row 1 K1M, [work row 1 of Chart, k4M] 6(7:7:8) times, work row 1 of Chart, k1M.

Row 2 P1M, [work row 2 of Chart, p4M] 6(7:7:8) times, work row 2 of Chart, p1M.

These 2 rows set the patt.

Cont in patt to end of row 17.

Next row Using M, purl to end, inc dec st at centre of row. *165(189:189:213) sts.*

Using M, work 1(3:5:7) row(s) St st.

Next row P4M, [1B, 5M] to last 5 sts, 1B, 4M.

Next row K3M, [1B, 1M, 1B, 3M] to end.

Next row P4M, [1B, 5M] to last 5 sts, 1B, 4M.

Dec row Using M, k7(5:4:7), [k2tog, k13(6:16:6)] 10(22:10:22) times, k2tog, k6(6:3:6). *154(166:178:190) sts.*

Using M, work 1(1:5:13) row(s) St st.

Divide for back and fronts

Next row K34(36:38:40), leave these sts on a spare needle for right front, cast off 7(9:11:13) sts, knit next 71(75:79:83) sts, leave these72(76:80:84) sts on a spare needle for back, cast off 7(9:11:13) sts, knit to end.

Cont on these 34(36:38:40) sts for left front.

Next row P4M, [1B, 5M] to last 6(8:4:6) sts, 1B, 5(7:3:5)M.

Next row K4(6:2:4) M, [1B, 1M, 1B, 3M] to end.

Chart 1

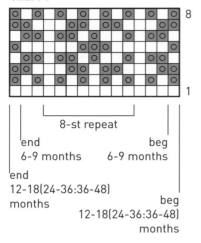

8-st repeat

end
6-9 months

beg
6-9 months

end
12-18(24-36:36-48)
months

beg
12-18(24-36:36-48)
months

Chart 3

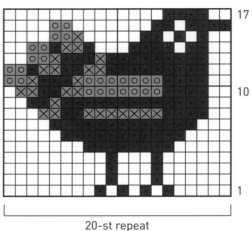

20-st repeat

Chart 2

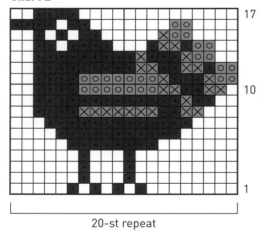

20-st repeat

Chart 4

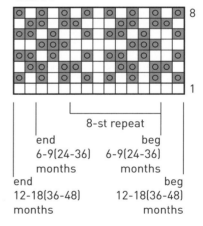

8-st repeat

end
6-9(24-36)
months

beg
6-9(24-36)
months

end
12-18(36-48)
months

beg
12-18(36-48)
months

Key

☐ Buckden (M)

■ Askrigg (A)

◉ Skipton (B)

☒ Richmond (C)

Next row P4M, [1B, 5M] to last 6(8:4:6) sts, 1B, 5(7:3:5)M.

Using M, work 1(3:5:7) row(s).

Work in patt from Chart 3.

Row 1 P7(8:9:10)M, work row 1 of Chart, p7(8:9:10)M.

Row 2 K7(8:9:10)M, work row 2 of Chart, k7(8:9:10)M.

These 2 rows set the patt.

Cont in patt to end of row 17.

Using M, work 1(3:5:7) row(s).

Next row P4M, [1B, 5M] to last 6(8:4:6) sts, 1B, 5(7:3:5)M.

Next row K4(6:2:4)M, [1B, 1M, 1B, 3M] to end.

Next row P4M, [1B, 5M] to last 6(8:4:6) sts, 1B, 5(7:3:5)M.

Cont in M only.

Shape neck

Row 1 Knit to last 3 sts, k2tog, k1.

Row 2 P1, p2tog, purl to end.

Dec one st at neck edge as set, on the next 10(11:12:13) rows. *22(23:24:25) sts.*

Work 2(3:4:5) rows.

Shape upper arm

Cast off 4 sts at beg of next and 2 foll right side rows. *10(11:12:13) sts.*

Work 1 row.

Next row Cast off 5 sts, knit to end.

Work 1 row.

Cast off rem 5(6:7:8) sts.

Back

With wrong side facing, rejoin yarn to centre 72(76:80:84) sts, cast on one st. *73(77:81:85) sts.*

Next row P3(5:4:6)M, [1B, 5M] to last 4(6:5:7) sts, 1B, 3(5:4:6)M.

Next row K2(4:3:5) M, [1B, 1M, 1B, 3M] to last 5(7:6:8) sts, 1B, 1M, 1B, 2(4:3:5) M.

Next row P3(5:4:6)M, [1B, 5M] to last 4(6:5:7) sts, 1B, 3(5:4:6)M.

Using M, work 1(3:5:7) row(s).

Work in patt from Chart 3.

Next row P8(9:10:11)M, work row 1 of Chart, p17(19:21:23)M, work row 1 of Chart, p8(9:10:11)M.

Next row K8(9:10:11)M, work row 2 of Chart, k17(19:21:23)M, work row 2 of Chart, k8(9:10:11)M.

These 2 rows set the motif.

Cont in patt to end of row 17.

Using M, work 1(3:5:7) row(s).

Next row P3(5:4:6)M, [1B, 5M] to last 4(6:5:7) sts, 1B, 3(5:4:6)M.

Next row K2(4:3:5) M, [1B, 1M, 1B, 3M] to last 5(7:6:8) sts, 1B, 1M, 1B, 2(4:3:5) M.

Next row P3(5:4:6)M, [1B, 5M] to last 4(6:5:7) sts, 1B, 3(5:4:6)M.

Cont in M only.

Work 14(16:18:20) rows.

Shape upper arms

Cast off 4 sts at beg of next 6 rows. *49(53:57:61) sts.*

Shape shoulders

Cast off 5 sts at beg of next 2 rows and and 5(6:7:8) sts at beg of foll 2 rows.

Leave rem 29(31:33:35) sts on a spare needle.

Right front

With wrong side facing, rejoin yarn to rem 34(36:38:40) sts.

Next row P5(7:3:5)M, [1B, 5M] to last 5 sts, 1B, 4M.

Next row K3M, [1B, 1M, 1B, 3M] to last 7(9:5:7) sts, 1B, 1M, 1B, 4(6:2:4)M.

Next row P5(7:3:5)M, [1B, 5M] to last 5 sts, 1B, 4M.

Using M, work 1(3:5:7) row(s).

Work in patt from Chart 3.

Row 1 P7(8:9:10)M, work row 1 of Chart, p7(8:9:10)M.

Row 2 K7(8:9:10)M, work row 2 of Chart, k7(8:9:10)M.

These 2 rows set the patt.

Cont in patt to end of row 17.

Using M, work 1(3:5:7) row(s).

Next row P5(7:3:5)M, [1B, 5M] to last 5 sts, 1B, 4M.

Next row K3M, [1B, 1M, 1B, 3M] to last 7(9:5:7) sts, 1B, 1M, 1B, 4(6:2:4)M.

Next row P5(7:3:5)M, [1B, 5M] to last 5 sts, 1B, 4M.

Cont in M only.

Shape neck

Row 1 K1, skpo, knit to end.

Row 2 Purl to last 3 sts, p2tog tbl, p1.

Dec one st at neck edge as set on the next 10(11:12:13) rows. *22(23:24:25) sts.*

Work 3(4:5:6) rows.

Shape upper arm

Cast off 4 sts at beg of next and 2 foll wrong side rows. *10 (11:12:13) sts.*

Shape shoulder

Work 1 row.

Next row Cast off 5 sts, purl to end.

Work 1 row.

Cast off rem 5(6:7:8) sts.

Sleeves

Using 3mm (US 2/3) needles and M, cast on 43(47:51:55) sts.

Moss st row (RS) K1, [p1, k1] to end.

This row forms the moss st.

Work a further 5(7:9:11) rows

Change to 3.25mm (US 3) needles.

Beg with a knit row, work in St st.

Work 2 rows.

Work rows 1–8 from Chart 4.

Using M work 2 rows, inc one st at centre of last row. *44(48:52:56) sts.*

Place motif

Row 1 K12(14:16:18)M, work across row 1 of Chart 2, k12(14:16:18)M.

Row 2 P12(14:16:18)M, work across row 2 of Chart 2, p12(14:16:18)M.

These 2 rows set the position for the Chart.

Cont in patt at the same time, inc one st at each end of the next and 3 foll 4th rows.

52(56:60:64) sts.

Work 3 rows to complete Chart.

Cont in M only, inc one st at each end on next and every foll 10th row until there are 58(64:70:76) sts.

Work straight until sleeve measures 17(21:25:29)cm/

6¾(8¼:9¾:11½)in from cast-on edge, ending with a wrong side row.

Mark each end of last row with a coloured thread.

Work a further 4(6:6:8) rows.

Cast off.

Front band and Collar

Join shoulder seams.

Using 3mm (US 2/3) needles, right side facing and M, pick up and k46(54:66:80) sts up right front to beg of neck shaping, 22(24:26:28) sts to shoulder seam, then k2(3:4:5), [m1, k4] 6 times, k3(4:5:6) across back neck sts, pick up and k22(24:26:28) sts to beg of neck shaping, turn. *125(139:157:177) sts.*

Work on last 79(85:91:97) sts only.

Row 1 P1, [k1, p1] 28(30:32:34) times, turn.

This row sets the moss st.

Row 2 Moss st to last 22(24:26:28) sts, turn.

Next 2 rows Moss st to last 20(21:22:23) sts, turn.

Next 2 rows Moss st to last 18 sts, turn.

Next 2 rows Moss st to last 15 sts, turn.

Next 2 rows Moss st to last 12 sts, turn.

Next 2 rows Moss st to last 9 sts, turn.

Next 2 rows Moss st to last 6 sts, turn.

Next row Moss st to last 3 sts, turn, moss st to end, pick up and k46(54:66:80) sts to cast-on edge. *171(193:223:257) sts.*

Moss st 3 rows across all sts.

Buttonhole row Moss st 4(5:4:4), rib 2tog, yrn, [rib 10(12:10:10) rib 2tog, yrn] 3(3:4:5) times, moss st to end.

Work 3 rows across all sts.

Cast off in moss st.

Making up

Join sleeve seams to coloured threads. Sew in sleeves. Sew on buttons.

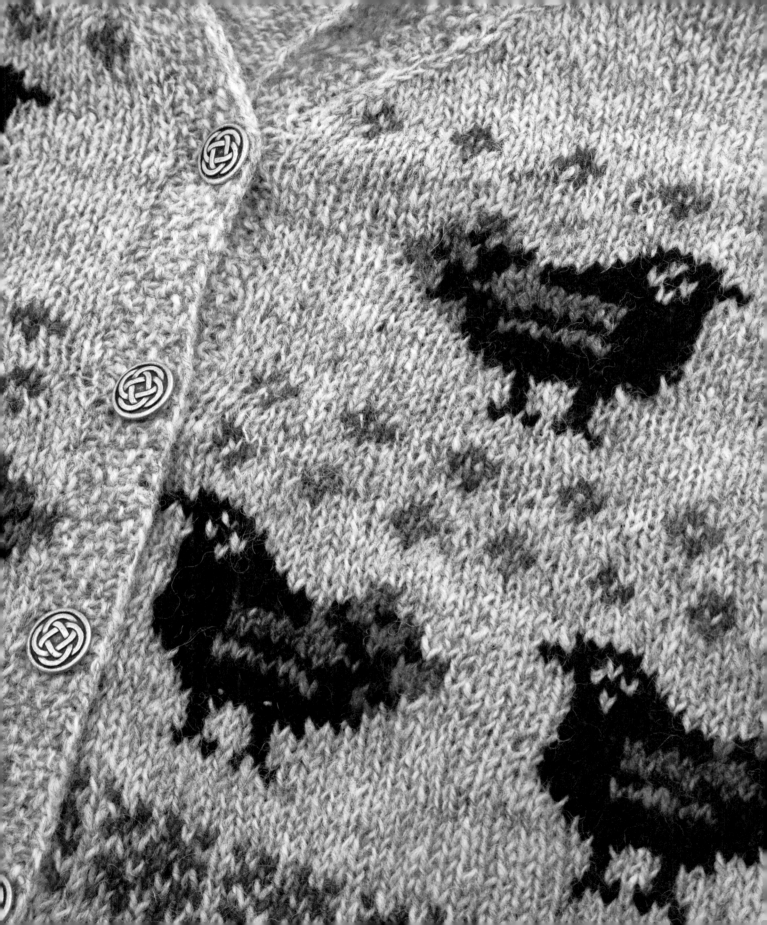

lotte scarf

The same little bird from the Lotte cardigan reappears in different colourways for this cosy but narrow scarf. Knitted in *Rowan Fine Tweed*.

Size

8cm/3in wide by 97(107:117:127)cm/
38(42:46:50)in long

Yarns

Rowan Fine Tweed
3(3:4:4) x 25g balls Nappa 380 (M)
One ball each Hubberholme 370 (A), Hawes 362 (B)
and Burnsall 375

Needles

Pair of 3.25mm (US 3) knitting needles

Tension

28 sts and 34 rows to 10cm/4in square over patt using
3.25mm (US 3) needles, *or size to obtain correct tension*.

Abbreviations

See page 141.

Note

When working from Charts, right side rows are read
from right to left and wrong side rows from left to
right.

Chart 1

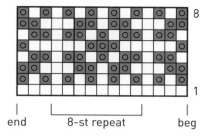

end   8-st repeat   beg

Chart 2

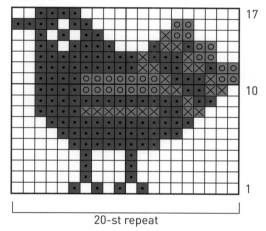

20-st repeat

Key

☐ Nappa (M)

■ Burnsall

⊙ Hubberholme (A)

⊠ Hawes (B)

To make (make 2 pieces)

Using 3.25mm (US 3) needles and M, cast on 47 sts.

Beg with a knit row, work in St st.

Work rows 1–8 from Chart 1.

Using M, work 2 rows and inc one st at centre of last row. *48 sts.*

Work in patt from Chart 2.

Row 1 K2M, work row 1 of Chart, k4M, work row 1 of Chart 2, k2M.

Row 2 P2M, work row 2 of Chart, p4M, work row 2 of Chart 2, p2M.

These 2 rows set the patt.

Cont in patt to end of row 17.

Next row Using M, purl to end and dec 3 sts across row. *45 sts.*

Using M, work 1(3:5:7) row(s) St st.

Next row P4M, [1A, 5M] to last 5 sts, 1A, 4M.

Next row K3M, [1A, 1M, 1A, 3M] to end.

Next row P4M, [1A, 5M] to last 5 sts, 1A, 4M.

Cont in M only until piece measures 48(53:58:63)cm/ 19(21:22¾:24¾)in.

Leave sts on a spare needle.

Making up

With needles pointing in the same direction and right sides together, cast off the sts of both pieces together.

Join row ends of scarf together.

With seam running down side of scarf, using 3.25mm (US 3) needles and B, working through both thicknesses, pick up and k24 sts along one short end.

Knit 2 rows.

Cast off.

Work other end to match.

sofie tunic

This very pretty tunic has a sweet heart motif on the front panel, a gently gathered skirt and a dropped neckline. It buttons at the shoulder. Knitted in Rowan *Wool Cotton 4 Ply* yarn. It looks great with either a skirt or trousers.

Sizes

To fit ages

6–9	12–18	24–36	36–48	months

Actual measurements

Chest

55	58	63	66	cm
21½	22¾	24¾	26	in

Length to shoulder

34	38	43	49	cm
13½	15	17	19¼	in

Sleeve length

17	21	25	29	cm
6¾	8¼	9¾	11½	in

Yarn

5(5:6:6) x 50g balls of Rowan *Wool Cotton 4 Ply* Violet 490

Needles

Pair each of 3mm (US 2) and 3.25mm (US 3) knitting needles
Cable needle

Extras

Stitch holders
3 buttons

Tension

28 sts and 36 rows to 10cm/4in square over St st on 3.25mm (US 3) needles, *or size to obtain correct tension.*

Abbreviations

K1tbl = knit through the back of the loop.

centre double increase [k1tbl, k1] into next st, then insert left-hand needle point behind the vertical strand that runs downward from between the 2 sts just made and k1tbl into this strand to make the 3rd st of the group.

Cr4R = slip next st onto cable needle and hold at back of work, k3, then p1 from cable needle.

Cr4L = slip next 3 sts onto cable needle and hold at front of work, p1, then k3 from cable needle.

Cr5R = slip next 2 sts onto cable needle and hold at back of work, k3, then p2 from cable needle.

Cr5L = slip next 3 sts onto cable needle and hold at front of work, p2, then k3 from cable needle.

Dec 7 = with yarn on RS of work, slip next 4 sts, *pass the 2nd st on right-hand needle over the first (centre) st, slip the centre st back onto left-hand needle and pass the 2nd st on left-hand needle over it *, slip the centre st back onto right-hand needle; rep from * to * twice more, knit the centre st.

See also page 141.

Note

When working from Chart, right side rows are read from right to left and wrong side rows from left to right.

Back

**Using 3mm (US 2) needles, cast on 119(125:137:143) sts.

Next row K1, [p1, k1] to end.

This row forms the moss st.

Work 5 more rows.

Change to 3.25mm (US 3) needles.

Beg with a knit row, work in St st until back measures 14(17:20:26)cm/5½(6¾:8 :10¼)in from cast-on edge, ending with a knit row.

Dec row [P2tog, p1] 39(41:45:47) times, p2tog.

*79(83:91:95) sts.***

Work straight until back measures 23(26:30:35)cm/

9(10¼:11¾:13¾)in from cast-on edge, ending with a wrong side row.

Shape armholes

Cast off 4(4:5:5) sts at beg of next 2 rows.

71(75:81:85) sts.

Next row K1, skpo, knit to last 3 sts, k2tog, k1.

Next row Purl to end.

Rep the last 2 rows 3(3:4:4) times more.

63(67:71:75) sts.

Cont straight until back measures 34(38:43:49)cm/13½(15:17:19¼)in from cast-on edge, ending with a wrong side row.

Shape shoulders

Rows 1 and 2 Cast off 7(8:8:9) sts, knit to last 7(8:8:9) sts, turn, purl to end.

Row 3 Cast off 8(8:9:9) sts, knit to last 15(16:17:18) sts, [k1, p1] 7(8:8:9) times, k1(0:1:0).

Row 4 K1(0:1:0), [p1, k1] 7(8:8:9) times.

Row 5 [K1, p1] 7(8:8:9) times, k1(0:1:0).

Rep the last 2 rows once more.

Cast off in patt.

Leave centre 33(35:37:39) sts on a holder.

Front

Work as Back from ** to **.

Work straight until front measures 16(19:23:28)cm/6¼(7½:9:11)in from cast-on edge, ending with a wrong side row.

Place heart motif

Row 1 K25(27:31:33), work across row 1 of Chart, k25(27:31:33).

Row 2 P25(27:31:33), work across row 2 of Chart, p25(27:31:33).

These 2 rows set the Chart position.

Working correct patt rows, cont straight until front measures 23(26:30:35)cm/9(10¼:11¾:13¾)in from cast-on edge, ending with a wrong side row.

Shape armholes

Cast off 4(4:5:5) sts at beg of next 2 rows.

71(75:81:85) sts.

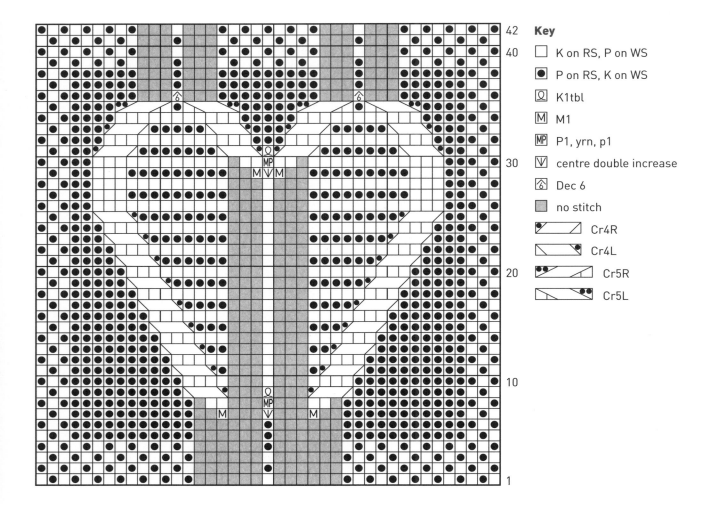

Key

☐	K on RS, P on WS
●	P on RS, K on WS
℧	K1tbl
M	M1
MP	P1, yrn, p1
V	centre double increase
⚅	Dec 6
▨	no stitch
╱	Cr4R
╲	Cr4L
╱	Cr5R
╲	Cr5L

Next row K1, skpo, patt to last 3 sts, k2tog, k1.

Next row Patt to end.

Rep the last 2 rows 3(3:4:4) times more. *63(67:71:75) sts.*
Cont straight working in St st when chart is completed
until front measures 30(34:38:44)cm/
11¾(13½:15:17¼)in from cast-on edge, ending with a
wrong side row.

Shape front neck

Row 1 K20(21:22:23), turn and work on these sts for first
side on neck shaping.

Row 2 P2tog, purl to end.

Row 3 Knit to last 2 sts, k2tog.

Rep the last 2 rows once more and row 2 again.
15(16:17:18) sts.

Work straight until 5 rows less have been worked than
on back to shoulder, ending with a right side row.

Shape shoulder

Rows 1 and 2 P7(8:8:9), turn, knit to end.

Buttonhole band

Row 3 [K1, p1] 7(8:8:9) times, k1(0:1:0).

Row 4 K1(0:1:0), [p1, k1] 7(8:8:9) times.

Rep the last 2 rows once more.

Buttonhole row K1, p1, yrn, k2tog, moss st 6, yrn, k2tog, moss st 3(4:5:6).

Work 2 rows.

Cast off in moss st.

With right side facing, slip centre 23(25:27:29) sts on a holder, rejoin yarn to rem 20(21:22:23) sts, knit to end.

Row 2 Purl to last 2 sts, p2tog tbl.

Row 3 Skpo, knit to end.

Rep the last 2 rows once more and row 2 again. *15(16:17:18) sts.*

Work straight until front measures the same as back to shoulder, ending at armhole edge.

Shape shoulder

Next row Cast off 7(8:8:9) sts, purl to end.

Work 1 row.

Cast off rem sts.

Sleeves

Using 3mm (US 2) needles, cast on 31(33:37:39) sts.

Next row P1, [k1, p1] to end.

This row forms the moss st.

Work 5 more rows.

Change to 3.25mm (US 3) needles.

Beg with a knit row, cont in St st.

Work 2 rows.

Inc row K3, m1, knit to last 3 sts, m1, k3.

Work 3 rows.

Rep the last 4 rows 11(12:14:15) times more and the inc row again. *57(61:69:73) sts.*

Cont straight until sleeve measures 17(21:25:29)cm/ 6¾(8¼:9¾:11½)in from cast-on edge, ending with a wrong side row.

Shape top

Cast off 4(4:5:5) sts at beg of next 2 rows. *49(53:59:63) sts.*

Next row K1, skpo, knit to last 3 sts, k2tog, k1.

Next row Purl to end.

Rep the last 2 rows 3(3:4:4) times more. *41(45:49:53) sts.*

Cast off.

Neckband

Join right shoulder seam.

With right side facing, using 3mm (US 2) needles, pick up and k16(16:18:18) sts down left side of front neck, k23(25:27:29) sts from front neck holder, pick up and k16(16:18:18) sts up right side of front neck, k33(35:37:39) sts from back neck, then pick up and k5 sts along buttonband. *93(97:105:109) sts.*

Moss st row K1, [p1, k1] to end.

Rep the last row once more.

Buttonhole row K1, p1, k1, p3tog, moss st to last 5 sts, p2tog, yf, k1, p1, k1.

Moss st 2 rows.

Cast off in moss st.

Making up

Lap buttonhole band over buttonband and tack together. Join side and sleeve seams. Sew in sleeves. Sew on buttons.

olle socks

Cosy socks in great stripes that make the most of any leftover *Felted Tweed DK* yarns, these are knitted top down on double-pointed needles.

Sizes
To fit ages

| 1–2 | 2–3 | 3–4 | years |

Yarns
40(50:60)g of leftover Rowan *Felted Tweed DK* in assorted colours

Needles
Set of 4 double-pointed needles (DPN) 3.25mm (US 3) and 3.75mm (US 5) needles
Spare needles
Stitch holder

Tension
24 sts and 30 rows to 10cm/4in over St st using 3.75mm (US 5) needles, *or size to obtain correct tension.*

Abbreviations
See page 141.

Note
Use the yarn for any stripe sequence you wish, we did 4 rows of each colour and chose one colour for the rib and heels.

Socks
Using 3.25mm (US 3) needles, cast on 40(44:48) sts.
Arrange these sts on 3 needles and cont in rounds.
Rib round *K1, p1; rep from * to end.
Rib a further 5(7:9) rounds.
Change to 3.75mm (US 5) needles.
Work in stripes of 4 rows each colour.
Knit 22(24:26) rounds.
Dec round K6, k2tog, knit to last 8 sts, skpo, k6.
38(42:46) sts.

Knit 7(9:11) rounds.

Dec round K5, k2tog, knit to last 7 sts, skpo, k5. *36(40:44) sts.*

Knit 7(9:11) rounds.

Dec round K4, k2tog, knit to last 6 sts, skpo, k4. *34(38:42) sts.*

Knit 7(9:11) rounds.

Dec round K3, k2tog, knit to last 5 sts, skpo, k3.

Knit 1 round. *32(36:40) sts.*

Break yarn.

Divide sts onto 3 needles as foll: slip first 9(10:11) sts onto first needle, next 7(8:9) sts onto second needle and next 7(8:9) sts onto 3rd needle, slip last 9(10:11) sts onto other end of first needle.

Shape heel

With right side facing, join yarn to 18(20:22) sts on first needle.

Work on these 18(20:22) sts only.

Beg with a knit row, work 10 rows St st.

Next row K13(15:17), skpo, turn.

Next row Sl 1, p8(10:12), p2tog, turn.

Next row Sl 1, k8(10:12), skpo, turn.

Next row Sl 1, p8(10:12), p2tog, turn.

Rep the last 2 rows twice more. *10(12:14) sts.*

Break yarn.

Reset sts on 3 needles as foll: slip first 5(6:7) sts of heel sts onto a stitch holder, place marker here to indicate beg of round.

Rejoin yarn to rem sts, with first needle k5(6:7), then pick up and k8 sts along side of heel, with 2nd needle k14(16:18), with 3rd needle pick up and k8 sts along other side of heel, k5(6:7) from stitch holder. *40(44:48) sts.*

Cont in rounds and stripe patt.

Knit 1 round.

Dec round K11(12:13), k2tog, k14(16:18), k2tog tbl, k11(12:13). *38(42:46) sts.*

Knit 1 round.

Dec round K10(11:12), k2tog, k14(16:18), k2tog tbl, k10(11:12). *36(40:44) sts.*

Knit 1 round.

Dec round K9(10:11), k2tog, k14(16:18), k2tog tbl, k9(10:11). *34(38:42) sts.*

Knit 1 round.

Dec round K8(9:10), k2tog, k14(16:18), k2tog tbl, k8(9:10). *32(36:40) sts.*

Work 20(28:36) rounds straight.

Shape toes

Dec round K5(6:7), k2tog, k2, skpo, k10(12:14), k2tog, k2, skpo, k5(6:7). *28(32:36) sts.*

Knit 1 round.

Dec round K4(5:6), k2tog, k2, skpo, k8(10:12), k2tog, k2, skpo, k4(5:6). *24(28:32) sts.*

Knit 1 round.

Dec round K3(4:5), k2tog, k2, skpo, k6(8:10), k2tog, k2, skpo, k3(4:5). *20(24:28) sts.*

Knit 1 round.

Dec round K2(3:4), k2tog, k2, skpo, k4(6:8), k2tog, k2, skpo, k2(3:4).

Knit 1 round. *16(20:24) sts.*

Slip first 4(5:6) sts onto one needle, next 8(10:12) sts onto next needle and rem 4(5:6) sts onto end of first needle.

Fold sock inside out and cast one st from each needle off together.

olle mittens

And here are the mittens to go with the socks. They're fun to knit and good for using up leftover balls of yarn. Make a few pairs in case they get lost or knit a string for them on a knitting dolly!

Sizes

To fit ages

| 1–2 | 2–3 | 3–4 | years |

Yarns

20(30:40)g of leftover Rowan *Felted Tweed DK* in assorted colours

Needles

Pair each of 3.25mm (US 3) and 3.75mm (US 5) knitting needles

Tension

24 sts and 30 rows to 10cm/4in over St st using 3.75mm (US 5) needles, *or size to obtain correct tension.*

Abbreviations

See page 141.

Note

Use the yarn for any stripe sequence you wish, we did 4 rows of each colour and chose one colour for the rib.

Right mitt

Using 3.25mm (US 3) needles, cast on 30(34:38) sts.
Rib row [K1, p1] to end.
Rep the last row 13 times more.
Change to 3.75mm (US 5) needles.
Cont in stripes of 4 rows.
Beg with a knit row, work 4 rows in St st.
Thumb shaping
Next row K15(17:19), m1, k2, m1, k13(15:17). *32(36:40) sts.*
Work 1 row.
Next row K15(17:19), m1, k4, m1, k13(15:17). *34(38:42) sts.*
Work 1 row.

Next row K15(17:19), m1, k6, m1, k13(15:17).
36(40:44) sts.
Work 1 row.
Next row K15(17:19), m1, k8, m1, k13(15:17).
38(42:46) sts.
Work 1 row.

2nd and 3rd sizes only
Next row K(17:19), m1, k10, m1, k(15:17). *(44:48) sts.*
Work 1 row.

3rd size only
Next row K(19), m1, k12, m1, k(17).
Work 1 row.

All sizes
38(44:50) sts.

Divide for thumb
Next row K25(30:35), turn, cast on 2 sts.
Next row P11(14:17) sts, turn, cast on 2 sts.
13(16:19) sts.
St st 8(10:12) rows.
Next row K1(0:1), * skpo; rep from * to end.
Next row Purl to end.
Break yarn, thread through rem sts, draw up tightly
and join seam.
With right side facing, pick up and k3(4:5) sts from
base of thumb, knit to end. *32(36:40) sts.***
St st 17(21:25) rows.

Shape top
Next row K2, [skpo, k9(11:13), k2tog, k2] twice.
28(32:36) sts.
Purl 1 row.
Next row K2, [skpo, k7(9:11), k2tog, k2] twice.
24(28:32) sts.
Purl 1 row.
Next row K2, [skpo, k5(7:9), k2tog, k2] twice.
20(24:28) sts.
Purl 1 row. Cast off.

Left mitt
Using 3.25mm (US 3) needles, cast on 30(34:38) sts.
Rib row [K1, p1] to end.

Rep the last row 13 times more.
Change to 3.75mm (US 5) needles.
Cont in stripes of 4 rows.
Beg with a knit row, work 4 rows in St st.

Thumb shaping
Next row K13(15:17), m1, k2, m1, k15(17:19).
32(36:40) sts.
Work 1 row.
Next row K13(15:17), m1, k4, m1, k15(17:19).
34(38:42) sts.
Work 1 row.
Next row K13(15:17), m1, k6, m1, k15(17:19).
36(40:44) sts.
Work 1 row.
Next row K13(15:17), m1, k8, m1, k15(17:19).
38(42:46) sts.
Work 1 row.

2nd and 3rd sizes only
Next row K(15:17), m1, k10, m1, k(17:19). *(44:48) sts.*
Work 1 row.

3rd size only
Next row K(17), m1, k12, m1, k(19). *50 sts.*
Work 1 row.

All sizes
38(44:50) sts.

Divide for thumb
Next row K22(26:30), turn, cast on 2 sts.
Next row P11(14:17) sts, turn, cast on 2 sts.
13(16:19) sts.
St st 8(10:12) rows.
Next row K1(0:1), * skpo; rep from * to end. *7(8:10) sts.*
Next row Purl to end.
Break yarn, thread through rem sts, draw up tightly
and join seam.
With RS facing, pick up and k3(4:5) sts from base of
thumb, knit to end. *32(36:40) sts.*
Work as given for right mitt from ** to end.

Making up
Join seam.

alexa poncho

Great for keeping warm, a hooded poncho is really easy to wear and can be layered over other sweaters. This one, in eye-catching pink, knitted in Rowan *Wool Cotton* is a real girlie treat. It has a lovely cabled edge for a finishing detail.

Sizes

To fit ages

6–9	12–18	24–36	36–48	months

Actual measurements

Cuff to cuff

61	71	81	89	cm
24	28	31¾	35	in

Length to shoulder

29	32	36	41	cm
11½	12½	14¼	16¼	in

Yarns

7(8:9:10) x 50g balls of Rowan *Wool Cotton* Flower 943

Needles

Pair each of 3.25mm (US 3) and 4mm (US 6) knitting needles
Long 4mm (US 6) circular needle
Cable needle

Tension

22 sts and 30 rows to 10cm/4in measured over St st using 4mm (US 6) needles, *or size to obtain correct tension.*

Abbreviations

C6B = slip next 3 sts onto cable needle and hold at back of work, k3, then k3 from cable needle.

C6F = slip next 3 sts onto cable needle and hold at front of work, k3, then k3 from cable needle.

C4R = slip next st onto cable needle and hold at back of work, k3, then p1 from cable needle.

C4L = slip next 3 sts onto cable needle and hold at front of work, p1, then k3 from cable needle.

C5R = slip next 2 sts onto cable needle and hold at back of work, k3, then p2 from cable needle.

C5L = slip next 3 sts onto cable needle and hold at front of work, p2, then k3 from cable needle.

MB = make bobble, [k1, p1, k1] all into next st, turn, p3, turn, k3, turn, p3, turn, sl 1, k2tog, psso.

C9B = slip next 4 sts onto cable needle and hold at back of work, k5, then k4 from cable needle.

See also page 141.

Note

When working from Charts, right side rows are read from right to left and wrong side rows from left to right.

Back

Using 4mm (US 6) circular needle, cast on 118(136:154:168) sts.

Foundation row (WS) P33(42:51:58), k2, p3, k5, p1, k2, [p6, k4] twice, p6, k2, p1, k5, p3, k2, p33(42:51:58).
Work in established patt.

Row 1 K33(42:51:58), work across row 1 of panel A, k1, panel B, k1, panel C, k33(42:51:58).

Row 2 P33(42:51:58), work across row 2 of panel C, p1, panel B, p1, panel A, p33(42:51:58).

These 2 rows set the panels and form the St st at sides. Work straight until back measures 29(32:36:41)cm/ 11½(12½:14¼:16¼)in from cast-on edge, ending with a wrong side row.

Panel A

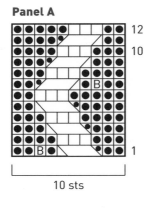

10 sts

Panel B

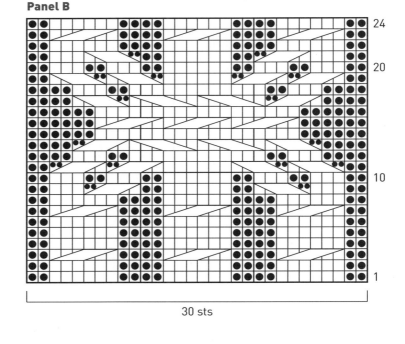

30 sts

Panel C

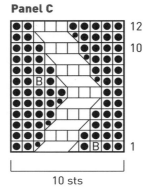

10 sts

Key

- ☐ K on RS, P on WS
- ⊡ P on RS, K on WS
- Ⓑ MB
- C4R
- C4L
- C5R
- C5L
- C6B
- C6F

Cast off 32(40:48:54) sts at beg of next 2 rows.

Cast off rem 54(56:58:60) sts, dec 6 sts over panel B.

Front

Work as given for back until front measures 22(25:28:33) cm/8¾(9¾:11:13)in from cast-on edge, ending with a wrong side row.

Front neck shaping

Next row Patt 44(53:62:69), turn and work on these sts for first side of neck shaping.

Next row Cast off 2 sts, patt to end.

Next row Patt to end.

Rep the last 2 rows 3(4:5:6) times more. *36(43:50:55) sts.*

Next row Work 2tog, patt to end.

Next row Patt to end.

Rep the last 2 rows 3(2:1:0) time(s) more.

32(40:48:54) sts.

Work straight until front measures the same as back, ending at side edge.

Cast off.

With right side facing, rejoin yarn to rem sts, dec 6 sts evenly, cast off centre 30 sts, patt to end.

Next row Patt to end.

Next row Cast off 2 sts, patt to end.

Next row Patt to end.

Rep the last 2 rows 3(4:5:6) times more.

36(43:50:55) sts.

Next row Work 2tog, patt to end.

Next row Patt to end.

Rep the last 2 rows 3(2:1:0) time(s) more.

32(40:48:54) sts.

Work straight until front measures the same as back, ending at side edge.

Cast off.

Hood

Using 4mm (US 6) needles, cast on 94(102:110:118) sts.

Beg with a knit row cont in St st until work measures 22(23:24:25)cm/8½(9:9½:10)in from cast-on edge, ending with a purl row.

Shape top

Next row K47(51:55:59), turn and work on these sts.

Next row Cast off 6 sts, purl to end.

Next row Knit to end.

Rep the last 2 rows 6 times more.

Cast off rem sts.

With right side facing, rejoin yarn to rem sts.

Next row Cast off 6 sts, knit to end.

Next row Purl to end.

Rep the last 2 rows 6 times more.

Cast off rem sts.

Cuffs

Join shoulder seams.

Place a marker 30(32:36:38) rows down from shoulder seams.

With right side facing, using 3.25mm (US 3) needles, pick up and k50(54:58:62) sts between markers.

Row 1 K2, [p2, k2] to end.

Row 2 P2, [k2, p2] to end.

Rep the last 2 rows for 7(8:9:10)cm/2¾(3¼:3½:4)in ending with row 1.

Cast off in rib.

Cable trim

Using 4mm (US 6) needles, cast on 11 sts.

Row 1 (RS) P2, k9.

Row 2 P9, k2.

Row 3 and 4 As rows 1 and 2.

Row 5 P2, C9B.

Row 6 As row 2.

Rows 7–12 Rep rows 1 and 2, three times.

These 12 rows form the patt.

Cont in established patt until trim fits around entire outer edge of poncho.

Cast off.

Work a further trim to fit round edge of hood.

Making up

Join cast-off edges of hood. Sew trim to row ends. Sew hood to neck edge. Join cuff seams. Placing cable edge at outer edge, begin and end at centre back, gather edging at corners so it remains flat, slip stitch in place.

josef waistcoat

Lots of small children like to have their arms free so this sleeveless textured short waistcoat is just the thing to wear over a cotton shirt. Knitted in Rowan *Wool Cotton 4 Ply* with a lovely chequerboard pattern.

Sizes

To fit ages

6–9	12–18	24–36	36–48	months

Actual measurements

Chest

55	59	63	67	cm
21½	23¼	24¾	26½	in

Length to shoulder

28	31	34	38	cm
11	12¼	13½	15	in

Yarn

2(3:3:4) x 50g balls of Rowan *Wool Cotton 4 Ply* Aqua 487

Needles

Pair each of 3mm (US 2/3) and 3.25mm (US 3) knitting needles
Circular 3mm (US 2/3) and 3.25mm (US 3) needles
Cable needle

Extras

4 buttons

Tension

28 sts and 36 rows to 10cm/4in square over St st using 3.25mm (US 3) needles, *or size to obtain correct tension.*

Abbreviations

C4F = slip next 2 sts onto cable needle and hold at front of work, k2, then k2 from cable needle.
C4R = slip next 2 sts onto cable needle and hold at back of work, k2, then p2 from cable needle.
C4L = slip next 2 sts onto cable needle and hold at front of work, p2, then k2 from cable needle.
See also page 141.

Note

When working from Chart, right side rows are read from right to left and wrong side rows from left to right.

Back and Fronts

(worked in one piece up to armholes)
Using 3mm (US 2/3) circular needle, cast on 145(157:169:181) sts.
Rib row 1 P1, [k1, p1] to end.
Rib row 2 K1, [p1, k1] to end.
Rep the last 2 rows 6(7:8:9) times more, inc one st at centre of last row. *146(158:170:182) sts.*
Change to 3.25mm (US 3) circular needle.
1st and 3rd sizes only
Row 1 (RS) P1, [work 24-st patt rep] 6(-:7:-) times, p1.
Row 2 Knit to end.
These 2 rows set the patt.
2nd and 4th sizes only
Row 1 (RS) P1, [work 24-st patt rep] 6(-:7:-) times, k12, p1.
Row 2 Knit to end.
These 2 rows set the patt.
All sizes
Cont in patt until work measures 18(20:22:25)cm/7(8:8¾:9¾)in from cast-on edge, ending with a wrong side row.

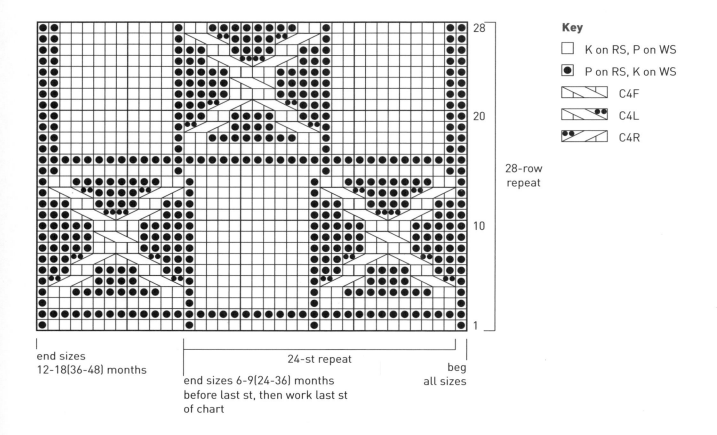

Key

□	K on RS, P on WS
⊙	P on RS, K on WS
⧄	C4F
⧄••	C4L
••⧄	C4R

28-row repeat

end sizes
12-18(36-48) months

24-st repeat

end sizes 6-9(24-36) months
before last st, then work last st
of chart

beg
all sizes

Divide for back and fronts

Next row Patt 31(33:35:37), leave these sts on a spare needle for right front, cast off next 10(12:14:16) sts, patt until there are 64(68:72:76) sts on the needle, turn and work on these sts for back, leave rem 41(45:49:53) sts on a spare needle for left front.

Next row Patt to end.

Next row K1, skpo, patt to last 3 sts, k2tog, k1.
Rep the last 2 rows 5 times more. *52(56:60:64) sts.*
Cont straight until work measures 28(31:34:38)cm/ 11(12¼:13½:15)in from cast-on edge, ending with a wrong side row.

Shape shoulders

Cast off 5(5:6:6) sts at beg of next 2 rows and 5(6:6:7) sts at beg of foll 2 rows.

Cast off rem 32(34:36:38) sts.

With right side facing, return to left front sts, cast off next 10(12:14:16) sts, patt to end. *31(33:35:37) sts.*

Next row Patt to end.

Next row K1, skpo, patt to last 3 sts, k2tog, k1.
Rep the last 2 rows 5 times more. *19(21:23:25) sts.*

Next row Patt to end.

Next row Patt to last 3 sts, k2tog, k1.
Rep the last 2 rows until 10(11:12:13) sts rem.
Work straight until front measures the same as back to shoulder, ending at armhole edge.

Shape shoulder

Next row Cast off 5(5:6:6) sts, patt to end.
Work 1 row.
Cast off rem sts.

With wrong side facing, return to right front sts, patt to end. *31(33:35:37) sts.*

Next row K1, skpo, patt to last 3 sts, k2tog, k1.

Next row Patt to end.

Rep the last 2 rows 5 times more. *19(21:23:25) sts.*

Next row K1, skpo, patt to end.

Next row Patt to end.

Rep the last 2 rows until 10(11:12:13) sts rem.

Work straight until front measures the same as back to shoulder, ending at armhole edge.

Shape shoulder

Next row Cast off 5(5:6:6) sts, patt to end.

Work 1 row.

Cast off rem sts.

Right front band and Collar

Using 3.25mm (US 3) circular needle, right side facing, pick up and k54(59:64:72) sts to beg of neck shaping, 45(48:51:57) sts to shoulder seam, then cast on 24(24:26:26) sts. *123(131:141:155) sts.*

Next 2 rows P1, [k1, p1] 12 times, turn, rib to end.

Next 2 rows Rib 29, turn, rib to end.

Next 2 rows Rib 33, turn, rib to end.

Next 2 rows Rib 37, turn, rib to end.

Next 2 rows Rib 41, turn, rib to end.

Next 2 rows Rib 45, turn, rib to end.

Cont in this way, working 4 more sts on each turning row for a further 12(14:14:16) rows.

Work 9 rows across all sts.

Cast off in rib.

Left front band and Collar

Using 3.25mm (US 3) circular needle, cast on 24(24:26:26) sts, then with right side facing, pick up and k45(48:51:57) sts to beg of neck shaping, 54(59:64:72) sts to cast-on edge. *123(131:141:155) sts.*

1st row P1, [k1, p1] to end.

This row sets the rib.

Next 2 rows Rib 25, turn, rib to end.

Next 2 rows Rib 29, turn, rib to end.

Next 2 rows Rib 33, turn, rib to end.

Next 2 rows Rib 37, turn, rib to end.

Next 2 rows Rib 41, turn, rib to end.

Next 2 rows Rib 45, turn, rib to end.

Cont in this way working 4 more sts on each turning row for a further 12(14:14:16) rows.

Work 3 rows across all sts.

Buttonhole row Rib 4, rib 2tog, y2rn, rib 2tog, [rib 8(8:10:12) rib 2tog, y2rn, rib 2tog] 3 times, rib to end.

Work 4 rows across all sts.

Cast off in rib.

Armbands

Join shoulder seams.

With right side facing, using 3mm (US 2/3) needles, pick up and k74(80:86:98) sts evenly round armhole edge.

Rib row [K1, p1] to end.

Rep the last row 4 times more.

Cast off in rib.

Making up

Sew row ends of back collar, sew cast-on edge to cast-off edge at back neck. Join side seams. Sew on buttons.

alphabet throw

Instant nostalgia comes with this lovely alphabet throw with traditional letters interspersed with Nordic reindeer and heart motifs. Knitted in Rowan *Felted Tweed DK* for a soft, cosy feel.

Size

60cm/23¾in by 105cm/41½in

Yarns

One 50g ball each of Rowan *Felted Tweed DK* Treacle 145, Rage 150, Bilberry 151, Watery 152, Phantom 153, Ginger 154, Pine 158, Gilt 160, Avocado 161, Seafarer 170, Clay 177, Horizon 179, Mineral 181, Peony 183

Needles

Pair of 3.75mm (US 5) knitting needles

Tension

23 sts and 32 rows to 10cm/4in square over St st using 3.75mm (US 5) needles, *or size to obtain correct tension.*

Abbreviations

See page 141.

Note

When working from Stag Chart, use the intarsia method. Use a small separate ball of yarn for each area of colour, twisting the yarns on wrong side when changing colour to avoid a hole.

When working from Heart and letter Charts, use the Fairisle method, strand the yarn not in use across the wrong side of work weaving them under and over the working yarn every 3 or 4 sts.

When working from Charts, right side rows are read from right to left and wrong side rows from left to right.

Motifs

Motif A (use 160 for letter)

Using 3.75mm (US 5) needles and 150, cast on 35 sts.

Row 1 K1, [p1, k1] to end.

Row 2 K1, [p1, k1] to end.

Row 3 K1, p1, k31, p1, k1.

Row 4 K1, purl to last st, k1.

These 2 rows form the St st with moss st borders.

Rows 5–15 Work as set.

Row 16 K1, p8, work across row 1 of motif, p8, k1.

Row 17 K1, p1, k7, work across row 2 of motif, k7, p1, k1.

Rows 18–32 Work from chart as set.

Row 33 K1, p1, k31, p1, k1.

Row 34 K1, purl to last st, k1.

Rows 35–45 Work as set.

Row 46 K1, [p1, k1] to end.

Row 47 K1, [p1, k1] to end.

Cast off in moss st.

Motif B (use 152 for letter)

Using 3.75mm (US 5) needles and 153, cast on 35 sts.

Row 1 K1, [p1, k1] to end.

Row 2 K1, [p1, k1] to end.

Row 3 K1, p1, k31, p1, k1.

Row 4 K1, purl to last st, k1.

These 2 rows form the St st with moss st borders.

Rows 5–15 Work as set.

Row 16 K1, p10, work across row 1 of motif, p10, k1.

Row 17 K1, p1, k9, work across row 2 of motif, k9, p1, k1.

Rows 18–32 Work from chart as set.

Row 33 K1, p1, k31, p1, k1.

Row 34 K1, purl to last st, k1.

Rows 35–45 Work as set.

Row 46 K1, [p1, k1] to end.

Row 47 K1, [p1, k1] to end.

Cast off in moss st.

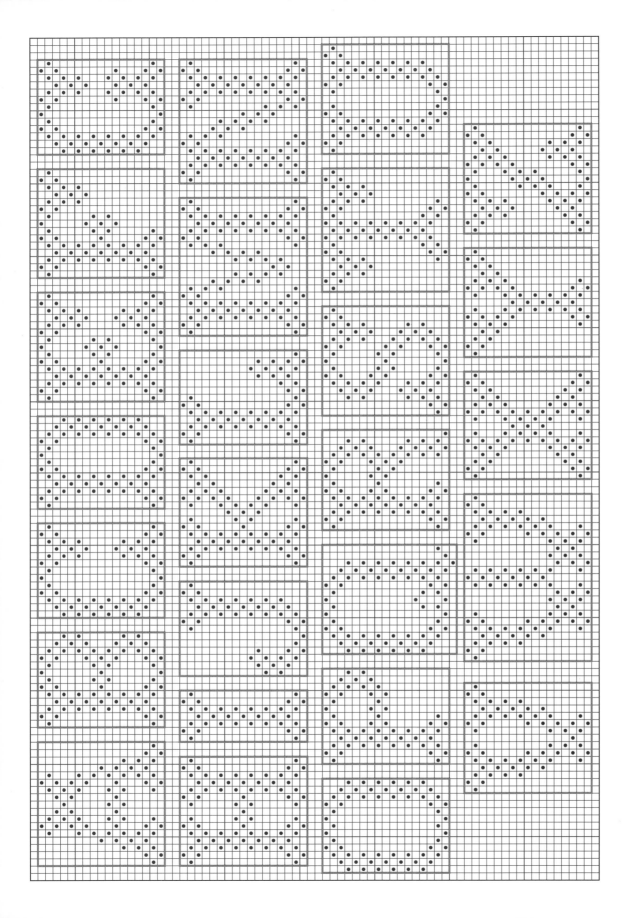

Key

☐ background colour

⊡ pattern colour

Motif C (use 170 for letter)
Using 3.75mm (US 5) needles and 177, cast on 35 sts.
Work as given for motif B.

Motif D (use 177 for letter)
Using 3.75mm (US 5) needles and 152, cast on 35 sts.
Work as given for motif B.

Motif E (use 181 for letter)
Using 3.75mm (US 5) needles and 170, cast on 35 sts.
Row 1 K1, [p1, k1] to end.
Row 2 K1, [p1, k1] to end.
Row 3 K1, p1, k31, p1, k1.
Row 4 K1, purl to last st, k1.
These 2 rows form the St st with moss st borders.
Rows 5–15 Work as set.
Row 16 K1, p9, work across row 1 of motif, p9, k1.
Row 17 K1, p1, k8, work across row 2 of motif, k8, p1, k1.
Rows 18–32 Work from chart as set.
Row 33 K1, p1, k31, p1, k1.
Row 34 K1, purl to last st, k1.
Rows 35–45 Work as set.
Row 46 K1, [p1, k1] to end.
Row 47 K1, [p1, k1] to end.
Cast off in moss st.

Motif F (use 145 for letter)
Using 3.75mm (US 5) needles and 183, cast on 35 sts.
Work as given for motif E.

Motif G (use 158 for letter)
Using 3.75mm (US 5) needles and 160, cast on 35 sts.
Work as given for motif B.

Motif H (use 145 for letter)
Using 3.75mm (US 5) needles and 161, cast on 35 sts.
Work as given for motif E.

Motif I (use 177 for letter)
Using 3.75mm (US 5) needles and 154, cast on 35 sts.
Row 1 K1, [p1, k1] to end.
Row 2 K1, [p1, k1] to end.
Row 3 K1, p1, k31, p1, k1.
Row 4 K1, purl to last st, k1.
These 2 rows form the St st with moss st borders.
Rows 5–15 Work as set.
Row 16 K1, p13, work across row 1 of motif, p13, k1.
Row 17 K1, p1, k12, work across row 2 of motif, k12, p1, k1.
Rows 18–32 Work from chart as set.
Row 33 K1, p1, k31, p1, k1.
Row 34 K1, purl to last st, k1.
Rows 35–45 Work as set.
Row 46 K1, [p1, k1] to end.
Row 47 K1, [p1, k1] to end.
Cast off in moss st.

Motif J (use 150 for letter)
Using 3.75mm (US 5) needles and 177, cast on 35 sts.
Work as given for motif B.

Motif K (use 183 for letter)
Using 3.75mm (US 5) needles and 151, cast on 35 sts.
Work as given for motif E.

Motif L (use 181 for letter)
Using 3.75mm (US 5) needles and 158, cast on 35 sts.
Work as given for motif B.

Motif M (use 170 for letter)
Using 3.75mm (US 5) needles and 179, cast on 35 sts.
Row 1 K1, [p1, k1] to end.
Row 2 K1, [p1, k1] to end.
Row 3 K1, p1, k31, p1, k1.
Row 4 K1, purl to last st, k1.
These 2 rows form the St st with moss st borders.
Rows 5–15 Work as set.
Row 16 K1, p7, work across row 1 of motif, p7, k1.

Row 17 K1, p1, k6, work across row 2 of motif, k6, p1, k1.
Rows 18–32 Work from chart as set.
Row 33 K1, p1, k31, p1, k1.
Row 34 K1, purl to last st, k1.
Rows 35–45 Work as set.
Row 46 K1, [p1, k1] to end.
Row 47 K1, [p1, k1] to end.
Cast off in moss st.

Motif N (use 160 for letter)
Using 3.75mm (US 5) needles and 150, cast on 35 sts.
Work as given for motif A.

Motif O (use 152 for letter)
Using 3.75mm (US 5) needles and 153, cast on 35 sts.
Work as given for motif B.

Motif P (use 170 for letter)
Using 3.75mm (US 5) needles and 177, cast on 35 sts.
Work as given for motif B.

Motif Q (use 177 for letter)
Using 3.75mm (US 5) needles and 152, cast on 35 sts.
Works rows 1–4 as motif E.
Row 15 K1, p1, k8, work across row 1 of motif, k8, p1, k1.
Row 16 K1, p9, work across row 2 of motif, p9, k1.
Row 17 K1, p1 k8, work across row 3 of motif, k8, p1, k1.
Rows 18–32 Work from Chart as set.
Complete as given for motif E.

Motif R (use 181 for letter)
Using 3.75mm (US 5) needles and 170, cast on 35 sts.
Works rows 1–15 as motif E.
Row 16 K1, p10, work across row 1 of motif, p9, k1.
Row 17 K1, p1 k8, work across row 2 of motif, k9, p1, k1.
Complete as given for motif E.

Motif S (use 145 for letter)
Using 3.75mm (US 5) needles and 183, cast on 35 sts.
Work as given for motif E.

Motif T (use 158 for letter)
Using 3.75mm (US 5) needles and 160, cast on 35 sts.
Work as given for motif A.

Motif U (use 145 for letter)
Using 3.75mm (US 5) needles and 161, cast on 35 sts.
Work as given for motif E.

Motif V (use 177 for letter)
Using 3.75mm (US 5) needles and 154, cast on 35 sts.
Work as given for motif E.

Motif W (use 150 for letter)
Using 3.75mm (US 5) needles and 177, cast on 35 sts.
Row 1 K1, [p1, k1] to end.
Row 2 K1, [p1, k1] to end.
Row 3 K1, p1, k31, p1, k1.
Row 4 K1, purl to last st, k1.
These 2 rows form the St st with moss st borders.
Rows 5–15 Work as set.
Row 16 K1, p5, work across row 1 of motif, p5, k1.
Row 17 K1, p1, k4, work across row 2 of motif, k4, p1, k1.
Rows 18–32 Work from chart as set.
Row 33 K1, p1, k31, p1, k1.
Row 34 K1, purl to last st, k1.
Rows 35–45 Work as set.
Row 46 K1, [p1, k1] to end.
Row 47 K1, [p1, k1] to end.
Cast off in moss st.

Motif X (use 183 for letter)
Using 3.75mm (US 5) needles and 151, cast on 35 sts.
Work as given for motif E.

Motif Y (use 181 for letter)
Using 3.75mm (US 5) needles and 158, cast on 35 sts.
Work as given for motif E.

Reindeer Motif

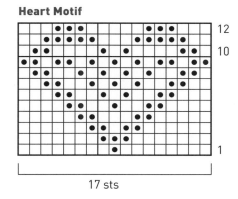

Heart Motif

17 sts

Key

☐ background colour

⊡ pattern colour

Motif Z (use 170 for letter)

Using 3.75mm (US 5) needles and 179, cast on 35 sts.

Work as given for motif E.

Reindeer Motif (use 170 for motif)

Using 3.75mm (US 5) needles and 161, cast on 35 sts.

Row 1 K1, [p1, k1] to end.

Row 2 K1, [p1, k1] to end.

Row 3 K1, p1, k31, p1, k1.

Row 4 K1, purl to last st, k1.

These 2 rows form the St st with moss st borders.

Rows 5–13 Work as set.

Row 14 K1, p8, work across row 1 of motif, p8, k1.

Row 15 K1, p1, k7, work across row 2 of motif, k7, p1, k1.

Rows 16–31 Work from chart as set.

Row 32 K1, purl to last st, k1.

Row 33 K1, p1, k31, p1, k1.

Rows 34– 45 Work as set.

Row 46 K1, [p1, k1] to end.

Row 47 K1, [p1, k1] to end.

Cast off in moss st.

Heart Motif (use 150 for motif)

Using 3.75mm (US 5) needles and 181, cast on 35 sts.

Row 1 K1, [p1, k1] to end.

Row 2 K1, [p1, k1] to end.

Row 3 K1, p1, k31, p1, k1.

Row 4 K1, purl to last st, k1.

These 2 rows form the St st with moss st borders.

Rows 5–17 Work as set.

Row 18 K1, p8, work across row 1 of motif, p8, k1.

Row 19 K1, p1, k7, work across row 2 of motif, k7, p1, k1.

Rows 20–29 Work from chart as set.

Row 30 K1, purl to last st, k1.

Row 31 K1, p1, k31, p1, k1.

Rows 32–45 Work as set.

Row 46 K1, [p1, k1] to end.

Row 47 K1, [p1, k1] to end.

Cast off in moss st.

Making up

Join motifs together to form a rectangle 4 squares wide by 7 squares long. Position motifs in alphabetical order with Reindeer motif between I and J and Heart motif between U and V.

alphabet blocks

The same alphabet letters, knitted in larger squares, are ideal for making a set of soft building blocks. You could make the child's name in letter blocks. Also knitted in Rowan *Felted Tweed DK*.

Size
15 x 15 x 15cm/6 x 6 x 6in

Yarns
One 50g ball each of Rowan *Felted Tweed DK* Rage 150, Phantom 153, Clay 177, Gilt 160, Watery 152, Seafarer 170

Needles
Pair of 3.75mm (US 5) knitting needles

Extras
Foam blocks each 15 x 15 x 15cm/6 x 6 x 6in

Tension
23 sts and 32 rows to 10cm/4in square over St st using 3.75mm (US 5) needles, *or size to obtain correct tension*.

Abbreviations
See page 141.

Note
When working from Charts, right side rows are read from right to left and wrong side rows from left to right.

To make
Each block is made by working six sides. We used the letters from the Alphabet Throw.

Making up
Leaving 3 sides open, make side into a cube. Insert foam block, join remaining seams.

morten jacket

This delightful Aran-inspired, heavily cabled jacket has a warm shawl collar. The cables run up the sleeves as well as on the fronts and back. It is knitted in *Rowan Fine Tweed*.

Sizes

To fit ages

6–9	12–18	24–36	36–48	months

Actual measurements

Chest

59	63	68	72	cm
23¼	24¾	26¾	28½	in

Length to shoulder

29	32	36	41	cm
11½	12½	14¼	16¼	in

Sleeve length

17	21	25	29	cm
6¾	8¼	9¾	11½	in

Yarn

9(10:11:12) x 25g balls of *Rowan Fine Tweed* Richmond 381

Needles

Pair of 3.25mm (US 3) knitting needles
Cable needle

Extras

4(4:5:5) buttons

Tension

28 sts and 36 rows to 10cm/4in square over St st using 3.25mm (US 3) needles.
36 sts and 38 rows to 10cm/4in square over cable patt using 3.25mm (US 3) needles.
Or size to obtain correct tension.

Abbreviations

Cr12fb = slip next 8 sts onto cable needle and leave at front of work, k4, then slip the last 4 sts to the left of cable needle back onto left-hand needle, take the cable needle to the back of work, k4 from left-hand needle, then k4 from cable needle.

Cr12bf = slip next 8 sts onto cable needle and leave at back of work, k4, then slip the last 4 sts to the left of cable needle, back onto left-hand needle, bring the cable needle to the front of work, k4 from left-hand needle, then k4 from cable needle.

See also page 141.

Note

When working from Chart, right side rows are read from right to left and wrong side rows from left to right.

Back

Using 3.25mm (US 3) needles, cast on 88(94:100:106) sts.

Row 1 (RS) P2(5:8:11), k4, [p2, k8, p2, k4] to last 2(5:8:11) sts, p2(5:8:11).

Row 2 K2(5:8:11), p4, [k2, p8, k2, p4], to last 2(5:2:5) sts, k2(5:8:11).

Row 3 (inc row) P2(5:8:11), k4, * p2, k1, m1, [k2, m1] 3 times, k1, p2, k4; rep from * to last 2(5:8:11) sts, p2(5:8:11). *47(50:53:56) sts.*

Row 4 K2(5:8:11), p4, [k2, p12, k2, p4] to last 2(5:8:11) sts, k2(5:8:11).

Cont in patt from chart.

Row 1 (RS) P2(5:8:11), k4, [work across row 1 of 20-st patt rep] 5 times, p2(5:8:11).

Row 2 K2(5:8:11), [work across row 2 of 20-st patt rep] 5 times, p4, k2(5:8:11).

These 2 rows **set** the cable panels.

Work straight until back measures 16(18:21:25)cm/6¼(7:8¼:9¾)in from cast-on edge, ending with a wrong side row.

Shape armholes

Cast off 1(2:3:4) st(s) at beg of next 2 rows.

106(110:114:118) sts.

Work straight until back measures 29(32:36:41)cm/11½(12½:14¼:16¼)in from cast-on edge, ending with a wrong side row.

Shape shoulders

Cast off 10 sts at beg of next 4 rows and 10(11:12:13) sts at beg of foll 2 rows.

Cast off rem 46(48:50:52) sts.

Left front

Using 3.25mm (US 3) needles, cast on 39(42:45:48) sts.

Row 1 (RS) P2(5:8:11), k4, [p2, k8, p2, k4] to last st, p1.

Row 2 K1, p4, [k2, p8, k2, p4], to last 2(5:8:11) sts, k2(5:8:11).

Row 3 (inc row) P2(5:8:11), k4, * p2, k1, m1, [k2, m1] 3 times, k1, p2, k4; rep from * to last st, p1. *47(50:53:56) sts.*

Row 4 K1, p4, [k2, p12, k2, p4] to last 2(5:8:11) sts, k2(5:8:11).

Cont in patt from chart.

Row 1 (RS) P2(5:8:11), k4, [work across row 1 of 20-st patt rep] twice, p1.

Row 2 K1, [work across row 2 of 20-st patt rep] twice, p4, k2(5:8:11).

These 2 rows **set** the cable panels.

Work straight until front measures 16(18:21:25)cm/6¼(7:8¼:9¾)in from cast-on edge, ending with a wrong side row.

Shape armhole and front neck

Next row Cast off 1(2:3:4) st(s), patt to last 3 sts, work 2tog, k1. *45(47:49:51) sts.*

Work 2 rows.

Next row K1, work 2tog, patt to end.

Work 2 rows.

Next row Patt to last 3 sts, work 2tog, k1.

Cont to dec in this way on every 3rd row until 30(31:32:33) sts rem.

Work straight until front measures same as back to shoulder, ending at armhole edge.

Shape shoulder

Cast off 10 sts at beg of next and foll right side row.

Work 1 row.

Cast off rem sts.

Right front

Using 3.25mm (US 3) needles, cast on 39(42:45:48) sts.

Row 1 (RS) P1, k4, [p2, k8, p2, k4] to last 2(5:8:11) sts, p2(5:8:11).

Row 2 K2(5:8:11), p4, [k2, p8, k2, p4], to last st, k1.

Row 3 (inc row) P1, k4, * p2, k1, m1, [k2, m1] 3 times, k1, p2, k4; rep from * to last 2(5:8:11) sts, p2(5:8:11). *47(50:53:56) sts.*

Row 4 K2(5:8:11), p4, [k2, p12, k2, p4] to last st, k1.

Cont in patt from chart.

Row 1 (RS) P1, [work across row 1 of 20-st patt rep] twice, k4, p2(5:8:11).

Row 2 K2(5:8:11), p4, [work across row 2 of 20-st patt rep] twice, k1.

These 2 rows **set** the cable panels.

Work straight until front measures 16(18:21:25)cm/ 6¼(7:8¼:9¾)in from cast-on edge, ending with a wrong side row.

Shape armhole and front neck

Next row K1, work 2tog, patt to end.

Next row Cast off 1(2:3:4) st(s) patt to end. *45(47:49:51) sts.*

Work 1 row.

Next row Patt to last 3 sts, work 2tog, k1.

Work 2 rows.

Next row K1, work 2tog, patt to end.

Work 2 rows.

Cont to dec in this way on every 3rd row until 30(31:32:33) sts rem.

Work straight until front measures same as back to shoulder, ending at armhole edge.

Shape shoulder

Cast off 10 sts at beg of next and foll wrong side row.

Work 1 row.

Cast off rem 10(11:12:13) sts.

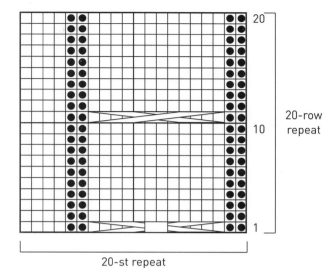

20-row repeat

20-st repeat

Key

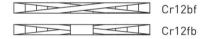

☐ K on RS, P on WS

▣ P on RS, K on WS

Cr12bf

Cr12fb

Sleeves

Using 3.25mm (US 3) needles, cast on 56(60:64:68) sts.

Row 1 (RS) P2(4:6:8), k4, [p2, k8, p2, k4] to last 2(4:6:8) sts, p2(4:6:8).

Row 2 K2(4:6:8), p4, [k2, p8, k2, p4], to last 2(4:6:8) sts, k2(4:6:8).

Row 3 (inc row) P2(4:6:8), k4, * p2, k1, m1, [k2, m1] 3 times, k1, p2, k4; rep from * to last 2(4:6:8) sts, p2(4:6:8). *68(72:76:80) sts.*

Row 4 K2(4:6:8), p4, [k2, p12, k2, p4] to last 2(4:6:8) sts, k2(4:6:8).

Cont in patt from chart.

Row 1 (RS) P2(4:6:8), k4, [work across row 1 of 20-st patt rep] 3 times, p2(4:6:8).

Row 2 K2(4:6:8), [work across row 2 of 20-st patt rep] 3 times, p4, k2(4:6:8).

These 2 rows **set** the cable panels.

Work a further 2(6:10:14) rows.

Inc row P2(4:6:8), m1, patt to last 2(4:6:8) sts, m1, p2(4:6:8).

Work 9 rows.

Rep the last 10 rows 3(4:4:5) times more and the inc row again, working all inc sts into rev St st. *78(84:88:94) sts.*

Work straight until sleeve measures 17(21:25:29)cm/ 6¾(8¼:9¾:11½)in from cast-on edge, ending with a wrong side row.

Mark each end of last row with a coloured thread.

Work a further 2(2:4:4) rows.

Cast off.

Right front band and Collar

Using 3.25mm (US 3) needles, right side facing, pick up and k45(51:57:67) sts to beg of neck shaping, 37(40:43:46) sts to shoulder seam, then cast on 16(19:22:25) sts. *98(110:122:138) sts.*

1st row P2, [k2, p2] 4(5:5:6) times, turn, rib to end.

Next 2 rows Rib 22(26:26:30), turn, rib to end.

Next 2 rows Rib 26(30:30:34), turn, rib to end.

Next 2 rows Rib 30(34:34:38), turn, rib to end.

Next 2 rows Rib 34(38:38:42), turn, rib to end.

Next 2 rows Rib 38(42:42:46), turn, rib to end.

Cont in this way working 4 more sts on each turning row for a further 6(8:10:12) rows.

Work 13 rows across all sts.

Cast off in rib.

Left front band and Collar

With 3.25mm (US 3) needles, cast on 16(19:22:25) sts, then with right side facing, pick up and k37(40:43:46) sts to beg of neck shaping, 45(51:57:67) sts to cast-on edge. *98(110:122:138) sts.*

1st row P2, [k2, p2] to end.

This row sets the rib.

Next 2 rows Rib 18(22:22:26), turn, rib to end.

Next 2 rows Rib 22(26:26:30), turn, rib to end.

Next 2 rows Rib 26(30:30:34), turn, rib to end.

Next 2 rows Rib 30(34:34:38), turn, rib to end.

Next 2 rows Rib 34(38:38:42), turn, rib to end.

Next 2 rows Rib 38(42:42:46), turn, rib to end.

Cont in this way working 4 more sts on each turning row for a further 6(8:10:12) rows.

Work 5 rows across all sts.

Buttonhole row Rib 4, rib 2tog, y2rn, rib 2tog, [rib 8(10:8:10) rib 2tog, y2rn, rib 2tog] 3(3:4:4) times, rib to end.

Work 6 rows across all sts.

Cast off in rib.

Making up

Join row ends of collar. Sew collar to back neck.

Sew in sleeves with last 2(2:4:4) rows to sts cast off at underarm. Join side and sleeve seams.

Sew on buttons.

mikal slipover

Another great textured design, this time with a split neck, which lends itself to layering. It is knitted in Rowan *Wool Cotton*.

Sizes

To fit ages

6–9	12–18	24–36	36–48	months

Actual measurements

Chest

55	58	64	68	cm
21¼	22¾	25	26¾	in

Length to shoulder

28	31	34	38	cm
11	12¼	13½	15	in

Yarn

2(3:3:4) x 50g balls of Rowan *Wool Cotton* Cypress 968

Needles

Pair each of 3.25mm (US 3) and 4mm (US 6) knitting needles

Extras

Stitch holders
2 buttons

Tension

25 sts and 30 rows to 10cm/4in square over St st using 4mm (US 6) needles, *or size to obtain correct tension.*

Abbreviations

K1tbl = knit through the back of the loop.
P1tbl = purl through the back of the loop.
See also page 141.

Note

When working from Chart, right side rows are read from right to left and wrong side rows from left to right.

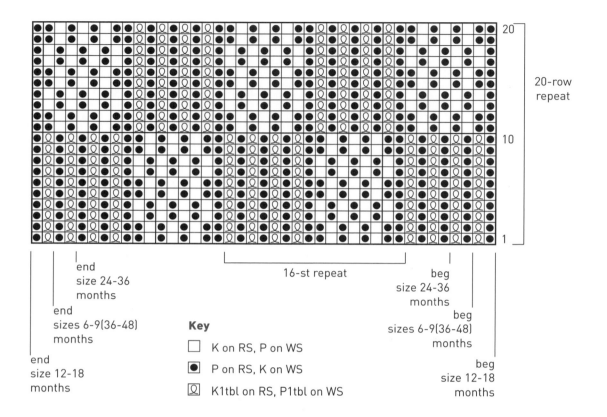

Key

☐ K on RS, P on WS

▣ P on RS, K on WS

Ⓠ K1tbl on RS, P1tbl on WS

20-row repeat

end size 24-36 months

end sizes 6-9(36-48) months

end size 12-18 months

16-st repeat

beg size 24-36 months

beg sizes 6-9(36-48) months

beg size 12-18 months

Back

Using 3.25mm (US 3) needles, cast on 69(73:81:85) sts.

Rib row 1 P1, [k1tbl, p1] to end.

Rib row 2 K1, [p1tbl, k1] to end.

Rep the last 2 rows 6(7:8:9) times more.

Change to 4mm (US 6) needles.

Work in patt from chart until back measures 18(20:22:25)cm/7(8:8¾:9¾)in from cast-on edge, ending with a wrong side row.

Shape armholes

Cast off 5(6:7:8) sts at beg of next 2 rows.

59(61:67:69) sts **.

Next row Skpo, patt to last 2 sts, k2tog.

Next row Patt to end.

Rep the last 2 rows 5(5:6:6) times more.

47(49:53:55) sts.

Cont straight until work measures 28(31:34:38)cm/ 11(12¼:13½:15)in from cast-on edge, ending with a wrong side row.

Shape shoulders

Cast off 5(5:6:6) sts at beg of next 2 rows and 5(6:6:7) sts at beg of foll 2 rows.

Leave rem 27(27:29:29) sts on a holder.

Front

Work as given for Back to **.

Next row Skpo, patt to last 2 sts, k2tog.

57(59:65:67) sts.

Divide for front opening

Next row Patt 25(26:29:30), turn, cast on 7 sts. *32(33:36:37) sts.*

Next row P1, [k1tbl, p1] 3 times, patt to last 2 sts, k2tog.

Next row Patt to last 7 sts, [k1, p1tbl] 3 times, p1.

Rep the last 2 rows 4(4:5:5) times. *27(28:30:31) sts.*

Work straight until front measures 23(25:28:31)cm/ 9(9¾:11:12¼)in from cast-on edge, ending with a wrong side row.

Shape front neck

Next row Patt 12(12:13:13), leave these sts on a holder, patt to end.

Dec one st at neck edge on every row until 10(11:12:13) sts rem.

Work straight until front measures the same as back to shoulder, ending at armhole edge.

Shape shoulder

Next row Cast off 5(5:6:6) sts, patt to end.

Work 1 row.

Cast off rem 5(6:6:7) sts.

Mark position for button halfway along front band.

Work buttonhole to match marker at same time as working left front as foll:

Buttonhole row (RS) Work to last 7 sts, p1, k1tbl, p1, k2tog, yf, k1tbl, p1.

With wrong side facing, rejoin yarn to rem sts, p1, [p1tbl, k1] 3 times, patt to end. *32(33:36:37) sts.*

Next row Skpo, patt to last 7 sts, [p1, k1tbl] 3 times, p1.

Next row P1, [p1tbl, k1] 3 times, patt to end.

Rep the last 2 rows 4(4:5:5) times. *27(28:30:31) sts.*

Work straight until front measures 23(25:28:31)cm/ 9(9¾:11:12¼)in from cast-on edge, ending with a wrong side row.

Shape front neck

Next row Patt to last 12(12:13:13) sts, leave these sts on a holder, turn.

Dec one st at neck edge on every row until 10(11:12:13) sts rem.

Work straight until front measures the same as back to shoulder, ending at armhole edge.

Shape shoulder

Next row Cast off 5(5:6:6) sts, patt to end.

Work 1 row.

Cast off rem 5(6:6:7) sts.

Neckband

Join shoulder seams.

With right side facing, using 3.25mm (US 3) needles, place 12(12:13:13) sts from holder onto needle, pick up and k12(12:14:14) sts up right side of front neck, k27(27:29:29) sts from back neck holder, pick up and k12(12:14:14) sts down left side of front neck, patt 8(8:9:9), k2tog, yf, k1tbl, p1 from left front holder. *75(75:83:83) sts.*

Row 1 P1, [p1tbl, k1] to last 2 sts, p1tbl, p1.

Row 2 P1, [k1tbl, p1] to end.

Row 3 As row 1.

Cast off in rib.

Armbands

With right side facing, 3.25mm (US 3) needles, pick up and k60(66:72:78) sts evenly around armhole edge.

Rib row 1 [P1tbl, k1] to end.

Rib row 2 [P1, k1tbl] to end.

Work 1 more row.

Cast off in rib.

Making up

Join side seams. Sew buttonband to back of buttonhole band. Sew on buttons.

aneka cardigan

A lovely traditional Aran cardigan for girls, this one is knitted in Rowan *Siena 4 Ply*, a cotton yarn that shows the cables and textures really beautifully as well as being easy to wear. Pretty heart buttons make a nice finishing touch.

Sizes

To fit ages

6–9	12–18	24–36	36–48	months

Actual measurements

Chest

55	59	63	67	cm
21½	23¼	24¾	26½	in

Length to shoulder

29	32	36	41	cm
11½	12½	14¼	16¼	in

Sleeve length

17	21	25	29	cm
6¾	8¼	9¾	11½	in

Yarn

4(5:5:6) x 50g balls of Rowan *Siena 4 Ply* Chilli 666

Needles

Pair each of 3mm (US 2/3) and 3.25mm (US 3) knitting needles
Cable needle

Extras

Stitch markers
6(6:7:7) buttons

Tension

28 sts and 36 rows to 10cm/4in square over St st using 3.25mm (US 3) needles, *or size to obtain correct tension*.

Abbreviations

C4B = slip next 2 sts onto cable needle and hold at back of work, k2, then k2 from cable needle.

C4F = slip next 2 sts onto cable needle and hold at front of work, k2, then k2 from cable needle.

Cr2R = slip next st onto cable needle and hold at back of work, k1, then p1 from cable needle.

Cr2L = slip next st onto cable needle and hold at front of work, p1, then k1 from cable needle.

MB = make bobble, [k1, p1, k1] in next st, turn, p3, turn, k3, turn, p3, turn, sl 1, k2tog, psso.

See also page 141.

Note

When working from Charts, right side rows are read from right to left and wrong side rows from left to right.

Back

Using 3mm (US 2/3) needles, cast on 93(99:105:111) sts.

Moss st row K1, [p1, k1] to end.

Rep the last row 7(9:11:13) times.

Change to 3.25mm (US 3) needles.

Row 1 (RS) Moss st 4(7:10:13), work across row 1 of panel A, B and A, moss st 7, work across row 1 of panel A, B and A, moss st 4(7:10:13).

Row 2 Moss st 4(7:10:13), work across row 2 of panel A, B and A, moss st 7, work across row 2 of panel A, B and A, moss st 4(7:10:13).

These 2 rows set the patt with moss st at sides and in the centre.

Work straight until back measures 16(18:21:25)cm/ 6¼(7:8¼:9¾)in from cast-on edge, ending with a wrong side row.

Shape armholes

Cast off 3(4:5:6) sts at beg of next 2 rows.
87(91:95:99) sts.

Work straight until back measures 29(32:36:41)cm/ 11½(12½:14¼:16¼)in from cast-on edge, ending with a wrong side row.

Shape shoulders

Cast off 8 sts at beg of next 4 rows and 8(9:10:11) sts at beg of foll 2 rows.

Cast off rem 39(41:43:45) sts.

Left front

Using 3mm (US 2/3) needles, cast on 53(56:59:62) sts.

Moss st row 1 K1(0:1:0), [p1, k1] to end.

Moss st row 2 [K1, p1] to last 1(0:1:0) st(s), k1(0:1:0).

Rep the last 2 rows 3(4:5:6) times.

Change to 3.25mm (US 3) needles.

Row 1 (RS) Moss st 4(7:10:13), work across row 1 of panel A, B and A, moss st 10.

Row 2 Moss st 10, work across row 2 of panel A, B and A, moss st 4(7:10:13).

These 2 rows set the patt with moss st at side and centre for front band.

Work straight until front measures 16(18:21:25)cm/ 6¼(7:8¼:9¾)in from cast-on edge, ending with a wrong side row.

Shape armhole

Next row Cast off 3(4:5:6) sts, patt to end.
50(52:54:56) sts.

Work straight until front measures 24(27:30:35)cm/ 9½(10¾:11¾:13¾)in from cast-on edge, ending with a wrong side row.

Shape neck

Next row Patt to last 17(18:19:20) sts, turn and place these sts on a holder.

Dec one st at neck edge on next 9 rows.
24(25:26:27) sts.

Work straight until front measures the same as back to shoulder, ending at armhole edge.

Shape shoulder

Cast off 8 sts at beg of next and foll right side row.

Work 1 row.

Cast off rem 8(9:10:11) sts.

Mark position for buttons, the first on the 5th row, the 6th(6th:7th:7th) on the first row of neck shaping and the rem 4(4:5:5) spaced evenly between.

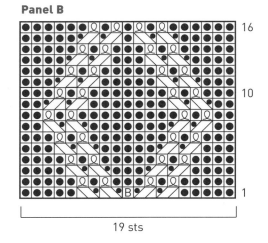

Panel A

8

1

10 sts

Panel B

16

10

1

19 sts

Key

☐	K on RS, P on WS
⬤	P on RS, K on WS
Ꝋ	K1tbl on RS, P1tbl on WS
B	MB
	Cr2R
	Cr2L
	C4B
	C4F

Right front

Using 3mm (US 2/3) needles, cast on 53(56:59:62) sts.

Moss st row 1 K1(0:1:0), [p1, k1] to end.

Moss st row 2 [K1, p1] to last 1(0:1:0) st(s), k1(0:1:0).

Rep the last 2 rows once more.

Buttonhole row Moss st 4, work 2tog, yrn, moss st to end.

Moss st 3(5:7:9) rows.

Change to 3.25mm (US 3) needles.

Row 1 (RS) Moss st 10, work across row 1 of panel A, B and A, moss st 4(7:10:13).

Row 2 Moss st 4(7:10:13), work across row 2 of panel A, B and A, moss st 10.

These 2 rows set the patt with moss st at side and centre for front band.

Working buttonholes to match markers, cont straight until front measures 16(18:21:25)cm/6¼(7:8¼:9¾)in from cast-on edge, ending with a right side row.

Shape armhole

Next row Cast off 3(4:5:6) sts, patt to end.

50(52:54:56) sts.

Work straight until front measures 24(27:30:35)cm/9½(10¾:11¾:13¾)in from cast-on edge, ending with a wrong side row.

Shape neck

Next row Moss st 4, work 2tog, yrn, moss st 4, patt 7(8:9:10) sts, place these 17(18:19:20) sts on a holder, patt to end.

Dec one st at neck edge on next 9 rows.

24(25:26:27) sts.

Work straight until front measures the same as back to shoulder shaping, ending at armhole edge.

Shape shoulder

Cast off 8 sts at beg of next and foll wrong side row.

Work 1 row.

Cast off rem 8(9:10:11) sts.

Sleeves

Using 3mm (US 2/3) needles, cast on 45(47:51:55) sts.

Moss st row K1, [p1, k1] to end.

Rep the last row 7(9:11:13) times.

Change to 3.25mm (US 3) needles.

Row 1 (RS) Moss st 3(4:6:8), work across row 1 of panel A, B and A, moss st 3(4:6:8).

Row 2 Moss st 3(4:6:8), work across row 2 of panel A, B and A, moss st 3(4:6:8).

These 2 rows set the patt with moss st at sides.

Work 0(4:8:12) rows.

Inc row Moss st 3(4:6:8), m1, patt to last 3(4:6:8) sts, m1, moss st 3(4:6:8).

Work 3 rows.

Rep the last 4 rows 11(13:14:15) times more and the inc row again, working all inc sts into moss st. *71(77:83:89) sts.*

Work straight until sleeve measures 17(21:25:29)cm/ 6¾(8¼:9¾:11½)in from cast-on edge, ending with a wrong side row.

Mark each end of last row with a coloured thread.

Work 2(4:6:8) rows.

Cast off.

Collar

Join shoulder seams.

With right side facing, using 3mm (US 2/3) needles, slip 17(18:19:20) sts from right front onto a needle, pick up and k20(20:22:22) sts up right side of front neck, 39(41:43:45) sts from back neck, 20(20:22:22) sts down left side of front neck, moss st 17(18:19:20) sts from left front neck holder. *113(117:125:129) sts.*

Work in moss st as set.

Next 2 rows Moss st to last 37(38:41:42) sts, turn.

Next 2 rows Moss st to last 33(33:36:37) sts, turn.

Next 2 rows Moss st to last 29(29:31:32) sts, turn.

Next 2 rows Moss st to last 25(25:26:27) sts, turn.

Next 2 rows Moss st to last 21(21:21:22) sts, turn.

Next 2 rows Moss st to last 17 sts, turn.

Next row Moss st to end.

Work 3 rows.

Cast off 10 sts at beg of next 2 rows. *93(97:105:109) sts.*

Change to 3.25mm (US 3) needles.

Work 20(20:22:22) rows.

Cast off in moss st.

Making up

Sew in sleeves with rows above coloured threads to sts cast off for armhole shaping.

Join side and sleeve seams. Sew on buttons.

bo cardigan

If you love knitting more challenging colourwork, this cardigan is the one to choose. With its fantastic design of little houses and hearts, and its traditional red and white colouring, it is a great modern take on traditional Scandinavian folk knitting. Knitted in *Rowan Fine Tweed*.

Sizes

To fit ages

6–9	12–18	24–36	36–48	months

Actual measurements

Chest

55	59	64	68	cm
21¾	23¼	25	26¾	in

Length to shoulder

31	33	38	42	cm
12¼	13	15	16½	in

Sleeve length

17	21	25	29	cm
6¾	8¼	9¾	11½	in

Yarns

Rowan Fine Tweed
5(5:6:6) x 25g balls Bainbridge 369 (A)
4 balls Bell Busk 376 (B)

Needles

Pair each of 2.75mm (US 2) and 3.25mm (US 3) knitting needles

Extras

Stitch holders
7 buttons

Tension

28 sts and 31 rows to 10cm/4in square over patt on 3.25mm (US 3) needles, *or size to obtain correct tension.*

Abbreviations

See page 141.

Note

When working from Charts, right side rows are read from right to left and wrong side rows from left to right. Use the Fairisle method and strand yarn across back of work over no more than 3 sts.

Working Back and Sleeves from Chart 1

For the size you are making, take off the centre st from the number of sts you have left, divide the remainder by 2 and count this number either side of the centre st, this will be your starting and finishing point.

Back

Using 2.75mm (US 2) needles and A, cast on 79(85:91:97) sts.
Rib row 1 K1, [p1, k1] to end.
Rib row 2 P1, [k1, p1] to end.
Rep the last 2 rows 5(6:6:7) times more.
Change to 3.25mm (US 3) needles.
Work in St st and patt from Chart 1.
1st size only
Beg at row 1 work to end of row 40.
2nd size only
Beg at row 37, work to end of row 40, then beg at row 1 work to end of row 40.
3rd size only
Beg at row 1, work to end of row 40, then work from row 1–14.
4th size only
Beg at row 37, work to end of row 40, then beg at row 1 work to end of row 40, then work from row 1–20.
All sizes
Row 1 Using B, knit to end.
Row 2 Using A, purl to end.
Row 3 K6(9:12:15)B, work across row 3 of Chart 2, k6(9:12:15)B.
Row 4 P6(9:12:15)B, work across row 4 of Chart 2, p6(9:12:15)B.
These 2 rows set the patt.
Cont in patt to end of row 31.
Cont in B only.
Work 11(13:17:19) rows.
Shape upper arms
Cast off 4 sts at beg of next 2 rows and 4(5:6:7) sts at beg of foll 2 rows. *63(67:71:75) sts.*
Cast off 7(8:8:9) sts at beg of next 2 rows and 8(8:9:9)

Chart 1

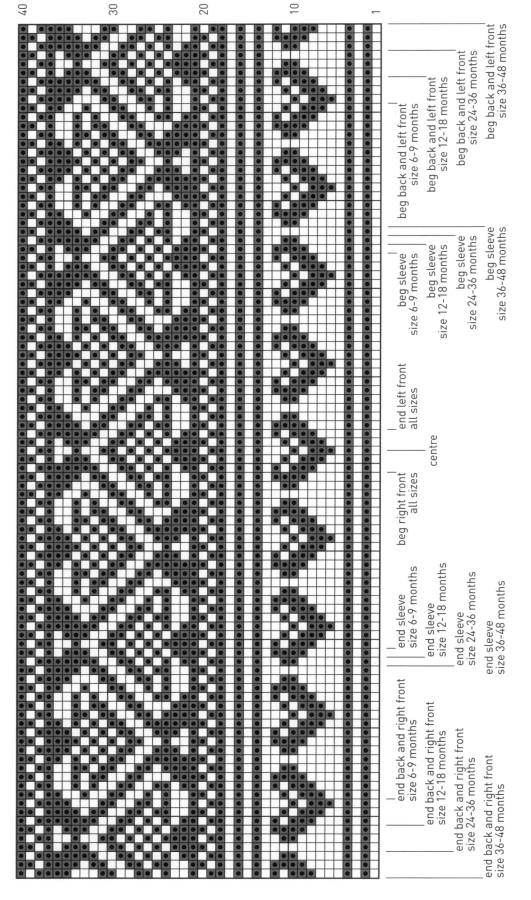

Key
- ● Bainbridge (A)
- □ Bell Busk (B)

Chart 2

Right Front (32 sts)

Left Front (37 sts)

Back (67 sts)

Key

■ Bainbridge (A)

☐ Bell Busk (B)

sts at beg of foll 2 rows.

Leave rem 33(35:37:39) sts on a holder.

Left front

Using 2.75mm (US 2) needles and A, cast on
37(39:43:45) sts.

Rib row 1 P1, [k1, p1] to end.

Rib row 2 K1, [p1, k1] to end.

Rep the last 2 rows 5(6:6:7) times more, inc one st at
centre of row on 2nd and 4th sizes only.
37(40:43:46) sts.

Change to 3.25mm (US 3) needles.

Work in St st and patt from Chart 1.

1st size only

Beg at row 1, work to end of row 40.

2nd size only

Beg at row 37, work to end of row 40, then beg at row 1
work to end of row 40.

3rd size only

Beg at row 1, work to end of row 40, then work from
row 1–14.

4th size only

Beg at row 37, work to end of row 40, then beg at row 1
work to end of row 40, then work from row 1–20.

All sizes

Row 1 Using B, knit to end.

Row 2 Using A, purl to end.

Row 3 K0(2:4:6)B, work first 37 sts of row 3 of Chart 2, k0(1:2:3)B.

Row 4 P0(1:2:3)B, work last 37 sts of row 4 of Chart 2, p0(2:4:6)B.

These 2 rows set the patt.

Cont in patt to end of row 31, then cont in B only **at the same time** when row 26 of chart has been worked, ending with a wrong side row.

Shape front neck

Next row Patt to last 6(7:8:9) sts, turn and leave these sts on a holder.

Dec one st at neck edge on every row until 23(25:27:29) sts rem.

Work straight until front measures the same as back to upper arm, ending at side edge.

Shape upper arm

Cast off 4 sts at beg of next row and 4(5:6:7) sts at beg of foll right side row. *15(16:17:18) sts.*

Shape shoulder

Work 1 row.

Cast off 7(8:8:9) sts at beg of next row.

Work 1 row.

Cast off rem 8(8:9:9) sts.

Right front

Using 2.75mm (US 2) needles and A, cast on 37(39:43:45) sts.

Rib row 1 P1, [k1, p1] to end.

Rib row 2 K1, [p1, k1] to end.

Rep the last 2 rows 5(6:6:7) times more, inc one st at centre of row on 2nd and 4th sizes only. *37(40:43:46) sts.*

Change to 3.25mm (US 3) needles.

Work in St st and patt from Chart 1.

1st size only

Beg at row 1, work to end of row 40.

2nd size only

Beg at row 37, work to end of row 40, then beg at row 1 work to end of row 40.

3rd size only

Beg at row 1, work to end of row 40, then work from row 1–14.

4th size only

Beg at row 37, work to end of row 40, then beg at row 1 work to end of row 40, then work from row 1–20.

All sizes

Row 1 Using B, knit to end.

Row 2 Using A, purl to end.

Row 3 K3(4:5:6)B, work last 32 sts of row 3 of Chart 2, k2(4:6:8)B.

Row 4 P2(4:6:8)B, work first 32 sts of row 4 of Chart 2, p3(4:5:6)B.

These 2 rows set the patt.

Cont in patt to end of row 31, then cont in B only **at the same time** when row 26 of Chart has been worked, end with a wrong side row.

Shape front neck

Next row Patt 6(7:8:9) sts, leave these sts on a holder, patt to end.

Dec one st at neck edge on every row until 23(25:27:29) sts rem.

Work straight until front measures the same as back to upper arm shaping, ending at side edge.

Shape upper arm

Cast off 4 sts at beg of next row and 4(5:6:7) sts at beg of foll wrong side row. *15(16:17:18) sts.*

Shape shoulder

Work 1 row.

Cast off 7(8:8:9) sts at beg of next row.

Work 1 row.

Cast off rem 8(8:9:9) sts.

Sleeves

Patt rows for sleeves

1st size only

Beg at row 1, work to end of row 40.

2nd size only

Beg at row 1, work to end of row 40, then work rows 1–14 again.

3rd size only

Beg at row 37, work to end of row 40, then work rows 1 to 40, then work from row 1–20.

4th size only

Beg at row 17, work to end of row 40, then beg at row 1 work to end of row 40, then work from row 1–14.

Using 2.75mm (US 2) needles and A, cast on 47(49:58:55) sts.

Rib row 1 K1, [p1, k1] to end.

Rib row 2 P1, [k1, p1] to end.

Rep the last 2 rows 5(5:6:6) times more.

Change to 3.25mm (US 3) needles.

Work in St st and patt from Chart, at the same time, inc one st at each end of the 3rd and 9(11:13:16) foll 4th rows. *67(73:81:89) sts.*

Work straight until all the rows have been worked.

Cast off.

Neckband

Join shoulder seams.

With right side facing, using 2.75mm (US 2) needles and B, place 6(7:8:9) sts from right front holder on needle, pick up and k19(21:23:25) sts up right side of front neck, k33(35:37:39) sts from back neck, pick up and k19(21:23:25) sts down left side of front neck, k6(7:8:9) from left front holder. *83(91:99:107) sts.*

Rib row 1 K1, [p1,k1] to end.

Rib row 2 P1, [k1, p1] to end.

Rep the last 2 rows twice more.

Break off B, join on A.

Work 1 row.

Cast off in rib.

Buttonband

With right side facing, using 2.75mm (US 2) needles and A, pick up and k66(72:80:87) sts evenly down front edge of left front.

Knit 4 rows.

Cast off.

Buttonhole band

With right side facing, using 2.75mm (US 2) needles and A, pick up and k68(72:80:87) sts evenly up front edge of right front.

Knit 1 row.

Buttonhole row K1(1:2:2), [k2tog, y2rn, skpo, k6(7:8:9)] 6 times, k2tog, y2rn, skpo, k1(1:2:3).

Knit 2 rows.

Cast off.

Making up

Sew on sleeves, placing centre of cast-off row to shoulder seam. Join side and sleeve seams. Sew on buttons.

folk bag

A cute small tote bag featuring little Scandinavian people, this would make a lovely present for a small girl. Knitted in Rowan *Felted Tweed DK*.

Size

Approx 20cm/8in wide by 20cm/8in deep

Yarns

Rowan *Felted Tweed DK*
2 x 50g balls Clay 177 (A)
One ball each Seafarer 170 (B), Avocado 161 (C) and Rage 150 (D)

Needles

Pair each of 3.25mm (US 3) and 3.75mm (US 5) knitting needles

Extras

Lining fabric 25 x 90cm/9¾ x 35½in
70cm/27½in of 2.5-cm/1-in wide petersham ribbon
Cardboard

Tension

26 sts and 26 rows to 10cm/4in square over patt using 3.75mm (US 5) needles, *or size to obtain correct tension.*

Abbreviations

See page 141.

Note

When working from Chart, right side rows are read from right to left and wrong side rows from left to right. Use the Fairisle method, strand the yarn not in use across the wrong side of work weaving them under and over the working yarn every 3 or 4 sts.

Front

Using 3.75mm (US 5) needles and A, cast on 54 sts.
Beg with a knit row, work in St st and patt from chart, working rows 1–46.
Change to 3.25mm (US 3) needles.
Knit 7 rows.
Cast off knitwise.

Back

Using 3.75mm (US 5) needles and A, cast on 54 sts.
Beg with a knit row, work in St st and patt from chart working rows 24–46, then rows 1–23.
Change to 3.25mm (US 3) needles.
Knit 7 rows.
Cast off knitwise.

Left gusset

Using 3.75mm (US 5) needles and A, cast on 15 sts.
Beg with a knit row, work 28 rows in St st.
Now work in patt from chart working rows 1–46.
Change to 3.25mm (US 3) needles.
Knit 7 rows.
Cast off knitwise.

Right gusset

Using 3.75mm (US 5) needles and A, cast on 15 sts.
Beg with a knit row, work 28 rows in St st.
Now work in patt from chart working rows 24–46, then rows 1–23.
Change to 3.25mm (US 3) needles.
Knit 7 rows.
Cast off knitwise.

Handles (make 2)

Using 3.75mm (US 5) needles and A, cast on 17 sts.
Next row K4, sl 1pw, k7, sl 1pw, k4.
Next row Purl to end.
Rep the last 2 rows 43 times more.
Cast off.

Making up

Using knitted pieces as a template and adding seam
allowance, cut out front, back and side gusset pieces
from lining.

Join cast-on edges of gussets.

Sew row ends of gusset to row ends and cast-on edges
of back and front. Make up lining in same way. Place
lining inside bag, fold seam allowance to wrong side
and slip stitch lining in place.

Cut petersham ribbon in half. Place petersham ribbon
along centre of wrong side of handle and slip stitch
in place along slipped sts. Bring row ends of handle
together encasing petersham ribbon and sew row
ends together. For extra stiffness in bottom of bag, cut
a piece of cardboard to fit bottom. From lining make a
'bag' to fit cardboard. Place in bottom of bag.

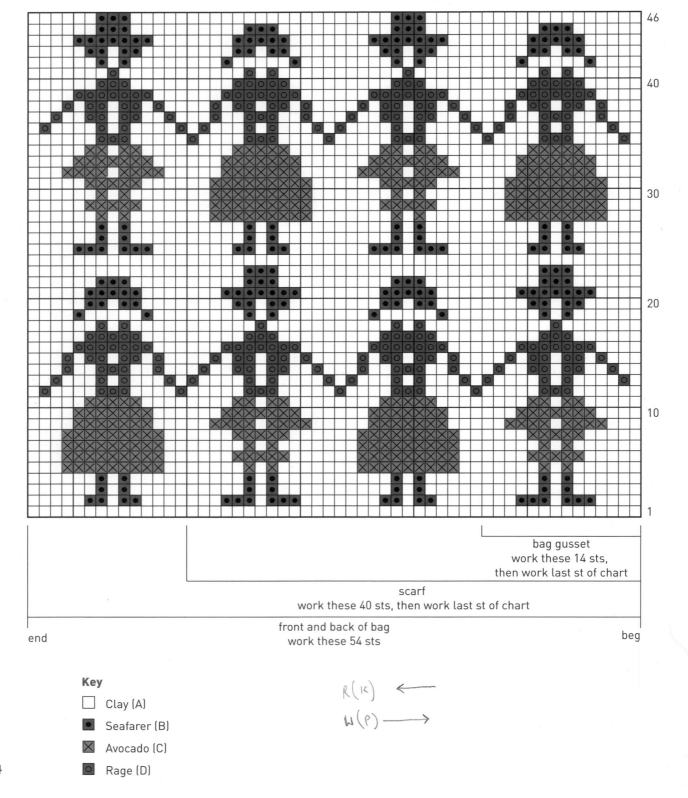

scarf
work these 40 sts, then work last st of chart

bag gusset
work these 14 sts,
then work last st of chart

front and back of bag
work these 54 sts

end

beg

R(K) ←

W(P) →

Key

☐ Clay (A)

▪ Seafarer (B)

☒ Avocado (C)

◉ Rage (D)

folk scarf

And here is the scarf
to accompany the
bag! Knitted in simple
stripes, it has the little
Scandinavian people
featured on the pockets
at each end. Also knitted
in Rowan *Felted Tweed DK*.

Size

Approx 15cm/6in wide by 142cm/56in long

Yarns

Rowan *Felted Tweed DK*
2 x 50g balls Clay 177 (A)
One ball each Seafarer 170 (B), Avocado 161 (C) and
Rage 150 (D)

Needles

Pair each of 3.25mm (US 3) and 3.75mm (US 5) knitting
needles

Tension

26 sts and 26 rows to 10cm/4in square over patt using
3.75mm (US 5) needles, *or size to obtain correct tension.*

Abbreviations

See page 141.

Note

When working from Chart, right side rows are read
from right to left and wrong side rows from left to
right. Use the Fairisle method, strand the yarn not
in use across the wrong side of work weaving them
under and over the working yarn every 3 or 4 sts.

Pocket (make 2)

Using 3.75mm (US 5) needles and A, cast on 41 sts.
Beg with a knit row, work in St st and patt from chart
working rows 1–46.
Change to 3.25mm (US 3) needles.
Cont in A only.
Row 47 K20, k2tog, k19. *40 sts.*
Row 48 P3, [k2, p2] to last 5 sts, k2, p3.
Row 48 Knit to end.
Rep the last 2 rows once more.
Cast off.

Scarf

Using 3.75mm (US 5) needles and A, cast on 80 sts.
Beg with a knit row, work in St st and stripes of 4
rows A, 4 rows D, 4 rows B, and 4 rows C until scarf
measures 141cm/55½in, ending 4 rows A.
Cast off.

Making up

With cast-on edges of pockets level with cast-on and
cast-off edges of scarf, sew one pocket centrally to
each end of scarf.
Join row ends of scarf together.
With seam running down centre of back, using
3.25mm (US 3) needles and D, working through both
thicknesses, pick up and k40 sts along one short end.
Knit 2 rows.
Cast off.
Work other end to match.

norse hat

And now one for the boys! A lovely beanie knitted in the traditional bird's-eye design with a contrasting coloured rib. Knitted in Rowan *Felted Tweed DK*.

Sizes

To fit 6–18 (24–48) months.
Circumference 42.5(47.5)cm/16¾(18¾)in

Yarns

One 50g ball each of Rowan *Felted Tweed DK* in Scree 165 (A), Seafarer 170 (B), Maritime 167 (C) and Ginger 154 (D)

Needles

Pair each of 3.25mm (US 3) and 3.75mm (US 5) knitting needles

Tension

23 sts and 28 rows to 10cm/4in square over patt using 3.75mm (US 5) needles, *or size to obtain correct tension.*

Abbreviations

See page 141.

To make

Using 3.25mm (US 3) needles and D, cast on 98(110) sts.
Row 1 P2, [k2, p2] to end.
Row 2 K2, [p2, k2] to end.
These 2 rows form the rib.
Work a further 8 rows.
Change to 3.75mm (US 5) needles.
Beg with a knit row, work in St st.
Row 1 Using B, work to end.
Row 2 Using B, work to end.
Row 3 Work 2B, [1A, 2B] to end.
Row 4 Using B, work to end.
Row 5 Using B, work to end.
Row 6 Using C, work to end.
Row 7 Using C, work to end.
Row 8 Work 2C, [1B, 2C] to end.
Row 9 Using C, work to end.
Row 10 Using C, work to end.

Row 11 Using A, work to end.
Row 12 Using A, work to end.
Row 13 Work 2A, [1C, 2A] to end.
Row 14 Using A, work to end.
Row 15 Using A, work to end.
These 15 rows form the stripe patt.
Work a further 15 rows.
Crown
Using B, beg with a knit row cont in St st only.
Work 2(6) rows, inc 3(1) st(s) evenly across last row. *101(111) sts.*
Shaping
Row 1 [K8(9), k2tog] 10 times, k1. *91(101) sts.*
Row 2 Purl to end.
Row 3 [K7(8), k2tog] 10 times, k1. *81(91) sts.*
Row 4 Purl to end.
Row 5 [K6(7), k2tog] 10 times, k1. *71(81) sts.*
Row 6 Purl to end.
Row 7 [K5(6), k2tog] 10 times, k1. *61(71) sts.*
Row 8 Purl to end.
Row 9 [K4(5), k2tog] 10 times, k1. *51(61) sts.*
Row 10 Purl to end.
Row 11 [K3(4), k2tog] 10 times, k1. *41(51) sts.*
Row 12 Purl to end.
Row 13 [K2(3), k2tog] 10 times, k1. *31(41) sts.*
Row 14 Purl to end.
Row 15 [K1(2), k2tog] 10 times, k1. *21(31) sts.*
2nd size only
Row 16 Purl to end.
Row 17 [K-(1), k2tog] 10 times, k1. *21 sts.*
Both sizes
Next row Purl to end.
Next row [K2tog] 10 times, k1. *11 sts.*
Next row Purl to end.
Break off yarn, thread through rem sts and fasten off.

Making up

Join seam.

norse scarf

The accompanying scarf to the hat, with matching contrast-coloured ribbed ends. Also knitted in Rowan *Felted Tweed DK*.

Size

13(14:15:16)cm/5(5½:6:6¼)in wide by 106(116:126:136)cm/41¾(45½:49½:53½)in long

Yarns

Rowan *Felted Tweed DK*
2 x 50g balls each Scree 165 (A), Seafarer 170 (B) and Maritime 167 (C)
One x 50g ball Ginger 154 (D)

Needles

Pair each of 3.25mm (US 3) and 3.75mm (US 5) knitting needles

Tension

23 sts and 28 rows to 10cm/4in square over patt using 3.75mm (US 5) needles, *or size to obtain correct tension.*

Abbreviations

See page 141.

To make

Using 3.75mm (US 5) needles and B, cast on 59(65:71:77) sts.
Beg with a knit row, work in St st.
Row 1 Using B, work to end.
Row 2 Using B, work to end.
Row 3 Work 2B, [1A, 2B] to end.
Row 4 Using B,work to end.
Row 5 Using B, work to end.
Row 6 Using C, work to end.
Row 7 Using C, work to end.

Row 8 Work 2C, [1B, 2C] to end.
Row 9 Using C, work to end.
Row 10 Using C, work to end.
Row 11 Using A, work to end.
Row 12 Using A, work to end.
Row 13 Work 2A, [1C, 2A] to end.
Row 14 Using A, work to end.
Row 15 Using A, work to end.
These 15 rows form the stripe patt.
Cont in patt until scarf measures 100(110:120:130)cm/39½(43¼:47¼:51)in, ending row 5.
Using B, cast off.

Making up

Join row ends together.
With seam running down centre of back, using 3.25mm (US 3) needles and D, working through both thicknesses, pick up and k30(34:34:38) sts along one short end.
Row 1 P2, [k2, p2] to end.
Row 2 K2, [p2, k2] to end.
These 2 rows form the rib.
Work a further 7 rows.
Cast off in rib.
Work other end to match.

lara sweater

This little cable and chequerboard pattern makes a sweet split-necked sweater for little girls. Knitted in Rowan *Cotton Glacé*, the stitch detail shows up beautifully.

Sizes

To fit ages

6–9	12–18	24–36	36–48	months

Actual measurements

Chest

52	58	65	72	cm
20½	22¾	25½	28¼	in

Length to shoulder

27	30	34	39	cm
10¾	11¾	13¼	15¼	in

Sleeve length

17	21	25	29	cm
6¾	8¼	9¾	11½	in

Yarn

4(5:5:6) x 50g balls of Rowan *Cotton Glacé* Sky 749

Needles

Pair each of 3mm (US 2/3) and 3.25mm (US 3) knitting needles
Cable needle

Extras

Stitch holders
3 buttons

Tension

30 sts and 40 rows to 10cm/4in square over patt using 3.25mm (US 3) needles, *or size to obtain correct tension.*

Abbreviations

C4B = slip next 2 sts onto cable needle and hold at back of work, k2, then k2 from cable needle.
C4F = slip next 2 sts onto cable needle and hold at front of work, k2, then k2 from cable needle.
See also page 141.

Note

When working from Chart, right side rows are read from right to left and wrong side rows from left to right. When there are not enough sts to work a cable, work these sts in St st.

Back

Using 3mm (US 2/3) needles, cast on 80(90:100:110) sts.
Rib row [K1, p1] to end.
Rep the last row 11(13:13:15) times more.
Change to 3.25mm (US 3) needles.
Row 1 (RS) Work last 3 sts of patt rep, [work across row 1 of patt rep] 7(8:9:10) times, work first 7 sts of patt rep.
Row 2 Work last 7 sts of patt rep, [work across row 2 of patt rep] 7(8:9:10) times, work first 3 sts of patt rep.
These 2 rows set the patt.
Cont in patt until back measures 15(17:20:24)cm/ 6(6¾:7¾:9½)in from cast-on edge, ending with a wrong side row.

Shape armholes

Cast off 8 sts at beg of next 2 rows. *64(74:84:94) sts.*
Work straight until back measures 27(30:34:39)cm/ 10½(11¾:13¼:15¼)in from cast-on edge, ending with a wrong side row.

Shape shoulders

Cast off 5(6:8:9) sts at beg of next 4 rows and 5(7:7:9) sts at beg of foll 2 rows.
Leave rem 34(36:38:40) sts on a holder.

Pocket linings (make 2)

Using 3mm (US 2/3) needles, cast on 16 sts.
Beg with a knit row, work 13(19:25:31) rows in St st.
Inc row P4, [m1, p3] 4 times. 20 sts.
Leave these sts on a holder.

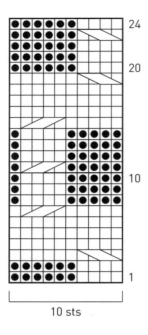

24

20

10

1

10 sts

Key

☐ K on RS, P on WS

⬤ P on RS, K on WS

▱ C4B

▱ C4F

Front

Work as given for back until 14(20:26:32) rows have been worked in patt.

Place pocket

Next row Patt 12(14:16:18), place next 20 sts on a holder, patt across 20 sts of first pocket lining, patt 16(22:28:34), place next 20 sts on a holder, patt across 20 sts of second pocket lining, patt 12(14:16:18).

Cont in patt until front measures 15(17:20:24)cm/ 6(6¾:7¾:9½)in from cast-on edge, ending with a wrong side row.

Shape armholes

Cast off 8 sts at beg of next 2 rows. *64(74:84:94) sts.*

Divide for front opening

Next row Patt 29(34:39:44), turn and work on these sts for first side of front.

Work straight until front measures 23(26:30:35)cm/ 9(10¼:11¾:13¾)in from cast-on edge, ending with a wrong side row.

Shape front neck

Next row Patt to last 7(8:9:10) sts, leave these sts on a holder, turn.

Dec one st at neck edge on every row until 15(19:23:27) sts rem.

Work straight until front measures the same as back to shoulder, ending at armhole edge.

Shape shoulder

Cast off 5(6:8:9) sts at beg of next and foll right side row. Work 1 row.

Cast off rem sts.

With right side facing, slip centre 6 sts on a holder, rejoin yarn to next st, patt to end.

Work straight until front measures 23(26:30:35)cm/ 9(10¼:11¾:13¾)in from cast-on edge, ending with a wrong side row.

Shape front neck

Next row Patt 7(8:9:10) sts, leave these sts on a holder, patt to end.

Dec one st at neck edge on every row until 15(19:23:27) sts rem.

Work straight until front measures the same as back to shoulder, ending at armhole edge.

Shape shoulder

Cast off 5(6:8:9) sts at beg of next and foll wrong side row.

Work 1 row.

Cast off rem sts.

Sleeves

Using 3mm (US 2/3) needles, cast on 40(44:48:52) sts.

Rib row [K1, p1] to end.

Rep the last row 11(13:13:15) times more.

Change to 3.25mm (US 3) needles.

Row 1 (RS) Work 3(5:2:4) sts of patt rep, [work across row 1 of patt rep] 3(3:4:4) times, work first 7(9:6:8) sts of patt rep.

Row 2 Work last 7(9:6:8) sts of patt rep, [work across row 2 of patt rep] 3(3:4:4) times, work first 3(5:2:4) sts of patt rep.

These 2 rows set the patt.

Inc and work into patt, one st at each end of the next and every foll 4th row until there are 66(74:82:88) sts.

Work straight until sleeve measures 17(21:25:29)cm/ 6¾(8¼:9¾:11½)in from cast-on edge, ending with a wrong side row.

Mark each end of last row with a coloured thread.

Work 10 rows.

Cast off.

Buttonband

Using 3mm (US 2/3) needles, cast on 9 sts.

Rib row 1 K2, p1, [k1, p1] twice, k2.

Rib row 2 [K1, p1] to last st, k1.

Rep the last 2 rows 14(16:18:20) times, leave these sts on a holder.

Buttonhole band

With right side facing, using 3mm (US 2/3) needles, work across sts at centre front as foll: k1, m1, k2, m1, k2, m1, k1. *9 sts.*

Rib row 1 [K1, p1] to last st, k1.

Rib row 2 K2, p1, [k1, p1] twice, k2.

Rep last 2 rows twice more and the first row again.

Buttonhole row Rib 4, yf, k2tog, rib 3.

Rib 11(13:15:17) rows.

Buttonhole row Rib 4, yf, k2tog, rib 3.

Rib 9(11:13:15) rows.

Do not fasten off.

Neckband

Join shoulder seams.

With right side facing, using 3mm (US 2/3) needles, rib 8 from buttonhole band, purl next st tog with first st on right front holder, k6(7:8:9), pick up and k17 sts up right side of front neck, k34(36:38:40) from back neck, pick up and k18 sts down left side of front neck, then purl next st tog with first st on buttonband, rib 8.

Next row Rib to end.

Buttonhole row Rib 4, yf, k2tog, rib to end.

Rib 3 rows.

Cast off in rib.

Making up

Sew in sleeves with last 10 rows to cast-off sts.

Join side and sleeve seams. Sew buttonband and buttonhole bands in place. Sew buttonband to back of buttonhole band. Sew on buttons.

finn sweater

This easy-to-wear sweater with a loose, slightly rolled neck is very comfortable. It features lovely textured stitches and a twisted cable design. Knitted in Rowan *Wool Cotton*.

Sizes

To fit ages

6–9	12–18	24–36	36–48	months

Actual measurements

Chest

52	59	66	73	cm
20½	23¼	26	28¾	in

Length to shoulder

27	30	34	39	cm
10¾	11¾	13½	15¼	in

Sleeve length

17	21	25	29	cm
6¾	8¼	9¾	11½	in

Yarns

6(6:7:7) x 50g balls of Rowan *Wool Cotton* Clear 941

Needles

Pair each of 3.75mm (US 5) and 4mm (US 6) knitting needles
Cable needle

Tension

22 sts and 30 rows to 10cm/4in square over St st using 4mm (US 6) needles.
25 sts sts and 36 rows to 10cm/4in square over patt using 4mm (US 6) needles.
Or size to obtain correct tension.

Abbreviations

C6B = slip next 3 sts onto cable needle and hold at back of work, k3, then k3 from cable needle.
See also page 141.

Back

Using 3.75mm (US 5) needles, cast on 70(78:86:94) sts.

Row 1 (RS) [K2, p2] 3(4:5:6) times, * k6, p2, [k2, p2] 3 times; rep from * once more, k6, [p2, k2] 3(4:5:6) times.

Row 2 [P2, k2] 3(4:5:6) times, * p6, k2, [p2, k2] 3 times; rep from * once more, p6, [k2, p2] 3(4:5:6) times.

Row 3 [K2, p2] 3(4:5:6) times, * C6B, p2, [k2, p2] 3 times; rep from * once more, C6B, [p2, k2] 3(4:5:6) times.

Row 4 [P2, k2] 3(4:5:6) times, * p6, k2, [p2, k2] 3 times; rep from * once more, p6, [k2, p2] 3(4:5:6) times.

Rows 5–10(10:14:14) Rep rows 1– 4 1(1:2:2) time(s), then rows 1 and 2 again.

Change to 4mm (US 6) needles.

Row 1 [K1, p1] 4(6:8:10) times, * k2, p2, C6B, p2, k2, [p1, k1] 3 times; rep from * once more, k2, p2, C6B, p2, k2, [p1, k1] 4(6:8:10) times.

Row 2 [K1, p1] 4(6:8:10) times, * p2, k2, p6, k2, p2, [k1, p1] 3 times; rep from * once more, p2, k2, p6, k2, p2, [p1, k1] 4(6:8:10) times.

Row 3 [K1, p1] 4(6:8:10) times, * k2, p2, k6, p2, k2, [p1, k1] 3 times; rep from * once more, k2, p2, k6, p2, k2, [p1, k1] 4(6:8:10) times.

Row 4 [K1, p1] 4(6:8:10) times, * p2, k2, p6, k2, p2, [k1, p1] 3 times; rep from * once more, p2, k2, p6, k2, p2, [p1, k1] 4(6:8:10) times.

These 4 rows form the patt.

Cont in patt until back measures 14(16:19:23)cm/ 5½(6¼:7½:9)in from cast-on edge, ending with a wrong side row.

Shape armholes

Cast off 4(5:6:7) sts at beg of next 2 rows.

62(68:74:80) sts.

Work straight until back measures 27(30:34:39)cm/ 10¾(11¾:13½:15¼)in from cast-on edge, ending with a wrong side row.

Shape shoulders

Cast off 5(6:7:8) sts at beg of next 4 rows and 5 sts at beg of foll 2 rows.

Leave rem 32(34:36:38) sts on a holder.

Front

Work as given for back until front measures 23(26:30:35)cm/9(10¼:11¾:13¾)in from cast-on edge, ending with a wrong side row.

Divide for neck

Row 1 Patt 21(23:25:27), turn and work on these sts.

Dec one st at neck edge on next 6 rows.

15(17:19:21) sts.

Work straight until front measures the same as back to shoulder, ending at armhole edge.

Shape shoulder

Next row Cast off 5(6:7:8) sts at beg of next and foll right side row.

Work 1 row.

Cast off rem sts.

With right side facing, place centre 20(22:24:26) sts on a holder, rejoin yarn to rem sts, patt to end.

21(23:25:27) sts.

Dec one st at neck edge on next 6 rows.

15(17:19:21) sts.

Work straight until front measures the same as back to shoulder, ending at armhole edge.

Shape shoulder

Next row Cast off 5(6:7:8) sts at beg of next and foll wrong side row.

Work 1 row.

Cast off rem sts.

Sleeves

Using 3.75mm (US 5) needles, cast on 34(34:42:42) sts.

Row 1 (RS) [K2, p2] 1(1:2:2) time(s), k6, p2, [k2, p2] 3 times, k6, [p2, k2] 1(1:2:2) time(s).

Row 2 [P2, k2] 1(1:2:2) time(s), p6, k2, [p2, k2] 3 times, p6, [k2, p2] 1(1:2:2) time(s).

Row 3 [K2, p2] 1(1:2:2) time(s), C6B, p2, [k2, p2] 3 times, C6B, [p2, k2] 1(1:2:2) time(s).

Row 4 [P2, k2] 1(1:2:2) time(s), p6, k2, [p2, k2] 3 times, p6, [k2, p2] 1(1:2:2) time(s).

Rows 5–10(10:14:14) Rep rows 1–4 1(1:2:2) time(s), then rows 1 and 2 again.

Change to 4mm (US 6) needles.

Row 1 [K1, p1] 0(0:2:2) times, k2, p2, C6B, p2, k2, [p1, k1] 3 times, k2, p2, C6B, p2, k2, [p1, k1] 0(0:2:2) times.

Row 2 [K1, p1] 0(0:2:2) times, p2, k2, p6, k2, p2, [k1, p1] 3 times, p2, k2, p6, k2, p2, [k1, p1] 0(0:2:2) times.

Row 3 [K1, p1] 0(0:2:2) times, k2, p2, k6, p2, k2, [p1, k1] 3 times, k2, p2, k6, p2, k2, [p1, k1] 0(0:2:2) times.

Row 4 [K1, p1] 0(0:2:2) times, p2, k2, p6, k2, p2, [k1, p1] 3 times, p2, k2, p6, k2, p2, [k1, p1] 0(0:2:2) times.

Inc and work into moss st, one st at each end of the next and every foll 4th row until there are 54(60:70:76) sts.

Work straight until sleeve measures 17(21:25:29)cm/ 6¾(8¼:9¾:11½)in from cast-on edge, ending with a wrong side row.

Mark each end of last row with a coloured thread.

Work a further 6(8:8:10) rows.

Cast off.

Neckband

Join right shoulder seam.

With right side facing, using 3.75mm (US 5) needles, pick up and k15 sts down left side of front neck, k20(22:24:26) from centre front neck holder, pick up and k15 sts up right side of front neck, k32(34:36:38) from back neck holder. *82(86:90:94) sts.*

Row 1 P2, [k2, p2] to end.

Row 2 K2, [p2, k2] to end.

Rep the last 2 rows twice more and the first row again.

Starting with a knit row, work 6 rows St st.

Cast off.

Making up

Join left shoulder and neckband.

Sew in sleeves with last 6(8:8:10) rows to cast-off sts.

Join side and sleeve seams.

tundra cushion

A lovely little cushion for the nursery with its pattern of differently shaped Nordic trees is knitted in Rowan *Felted Tweed DK*, making it beautifully soft. A treat for anyone who enjoys colourwork knitting!

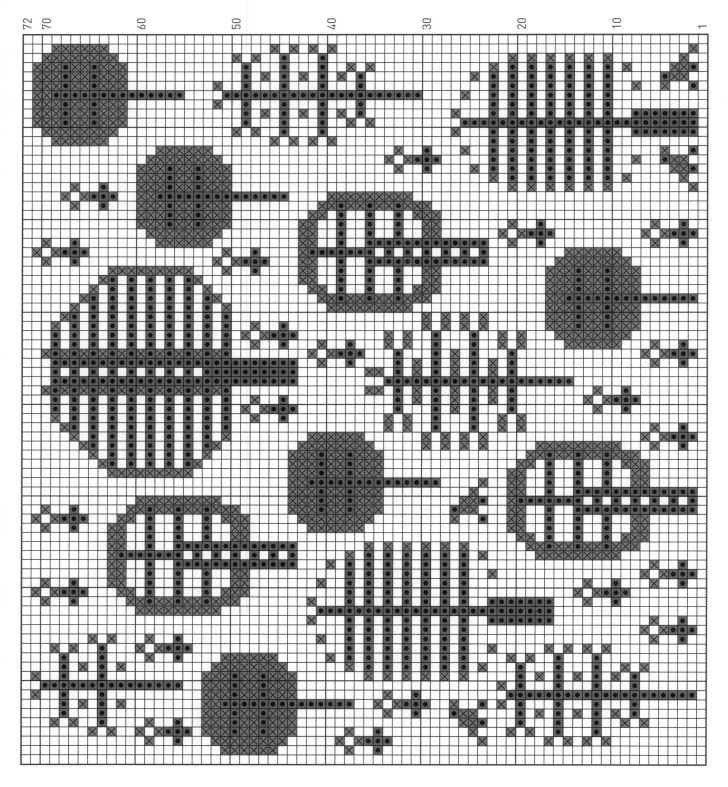

Key

☐ Clay (A)

▣ Pine (B)

⊠ Avocado (C)

Size

30 x 30cm/11¾ x 11¾in

Yarns

One 50g ball each of Rowan *Felted Tweed DK* Clay 177
(A), Pine 158 (B) and Avocado 161 (C)

Needles

Pair each of 3.75mm (US 5) and 4mm (US 6) knitting
needles

Extras

25cm/10in zip
Cushion pad

Tension

22 sts and 28 rows to 10cm/4in square over St st using
4mm (US 6) needles.
26 sts and 24 rows to 10cm/4in square over St st and
patt using 3.75mm (US 5) needles.
Or size to obtain correct tension.

Abbreviations

See page 141.

Note

When working from Chart, right side rows are read
from right to left and wrong side rows from left to
right.

Front

Using 3.75mm (US 5) needles and A, cast on 79 sts.
Using a combination of Fairisle and intarsia, beg with
a knit row, work in St st and patt from chart to end of
row 72.
Using A, cast off.

Back

Lower back

Using 4mm (US 6) needles and A, cast on 66 sts.
Beg with a knit row work 60 rows in St st and stripes of
4 rows A, 4 rows B and 4 rows C.
Using C, cast off.

Upper back

Using 4mm (US 6) needles and A, cast on 66 sts.
Beg with a knit row, work 24 rows in St st and stripes
of 4 rows A, 4 rows B and 4 rows C.
Using C, cast off.

Making up

Leaving 25cm/10in opening for zip, sew upper back to
lower back. Sew in zip. With right sides together, sew
back to front. Turn to right side.
Insert cushion pad.

pattern information

Sizing

The instructions in the patterns are given for the smallest size first, and larger sizes follow in parentheses. If there is only one set of figures, it refers to all sizes. If - (hyphen) or 0 (zero) is given in an instruction for the size you are knitting, then that particular instruction does not apply to your size.

Tension

The correct tension can make the difference between a successful garment and a disastrous one. It controls both the shape and size of an article, so any variation, however slight, can distort the finished garment.

You must match the tension given at the start of each pattern. To check your tension, knit a square in the pattern stitch and/or stocking stitch of perhaps 5–10 more stitches and 5–10 more rows than those given in the tension note. Press the finished square under a damp cloth and mark out the central 10cm/4in square with pins. If you have too many stitches to 10cm/4in, try again using thicker needles. If you have too few stitches to 10cm/4in, try again using finer needles. Once you have achieved the correct tension, your garment will be knitted to the right size.

Cable patterns

Cable stitch patterns allow you to twist the stitches in various ways, to create decorative effects such as an interesting rope-like structure to the knitting. The cables can be thin and fine (just a couple of stitches wide) or really big and chunky (up to 8 stitches or more).

To work cables, you need to hold the appropriate number of stitches that form the cable twist (abbreviated in pattern as C) on a separate small cable needle, while you knit behind or in front of them. You then knit the stitches off the cable needle before continuing to knit the remaining stitches in the row.

Depending on whether the cable needle is at the front or the back of the work, the cables will twist to the left or right but the principle remains the same. A four-stitch cable will be abbreviated as C4F or C4B depending on whether the cable needle is held to the front or back of the work.

Colourwork knitting

There are two main methods of working with colour in knitted fabrics: the intarsia and the Fairisle techniques. The first method produces a single thickness of fabric and is usually used where a new colour is required for a block of stitches and rows in a particular area of a piece of knitting. Where a small repeating colour pattern of up to 3 or 4 stitches is created across the row, the Fairisle technique is generally used.

Intarsia

For this technique, you join in a new yarn colour for each new block of colour stitches. To prevent the yarns getting twisted on the ball, the simplest method is to make individual little balls of yarn, or bobbins, from pre-cut short lengths of yarn, one for each motif or block of colour used in a row. You then work across the stitches, joining in the colours as required, by twisting them around each other where they meet on the wrong side of the work, to avoid gaps. After you have completed the piece of knitting, you need to neaten the loose ends. They can either be darned along the colour joins, or they can be knitted in to the fabric as each colour is worked by picking up the loops of the yarns carried across the back of the work as you knit.

Fairisle

When you are working a pattern with two or more repeating colours in the same row, you need to strand the yarn not in use behind the stitches being worked.

This needs to be done with care, loosely enough to ensure that the strands not in work do not tighten and pucker the front of the knitting. To do this, treat the yarns not in use (known as 'floating yarns') as if they were one yarn and spread the stitches as you work to their correct width to keep them elastic. If your pattern demands that the stranded or floating yarns are carried across more than three stitches, it is wise to weave the new yarn colour under and over the colour yarn you are working with each time you change colours (over the first time, under the second time and so on). The alternating 'under and over' movement helps to prevent the floating yarns from tangling by keeping them caught at the back of the work.

It is important when knitting with more than one colour to keep your tension correct, as it easy to pull the loops of yarn too tight, puckering the work. If you tend to knit colourwork too tightly, increase your needle size for the colourwork section.

Finishing methods

Pressing

Block out each piece of knitting by pinning it on a board to the correct measurements in the pattern. Then lightly press it according to the ball band instructions, omitting any ribbed areas. Take special care to press the edges, as this makes sewing up easier and neater. If you cannot press the fabric, then cover the knitted fabric with a damp cloth and allow it to stand for a couple of hours.

Darn in all ends neatly along the selvedge edge or a colour join, as appropriate.

Stitching seams

When you stitch the pieces together, match any areas of colour and texture carefully where they meet. Use a special seam stitch, called mattress stitch, as it creates the flattest seam. When complete, press the seams and hems. Lastly, sew on the buttons to correspond with the positions of the buttonholes.

Abbreviations

alt	alternate
approx	approximately
beg	begin(s)(ning)
cm	centimetres
cont	continu(e)(ing)
dec	decreas(e)(ing)
DPN	double-pointed needle
foll	follow(s)(ing)
g	gram
in	inch(es)
inc	increas(e)(ing)
k	knit
k2tog	knit next 2 stitches together
m1	make one stitch by picking up horizontal loop before next stitch and knitting into back of it
m	metres
p	purl
patt	pattern
psso	pass slipped stitch over
p2tog	purl next 2 stitches together
p3tog	purl next 3 stitches together
rem	remain(s)(ing)
rep	repeat
rev St st	reverse stocking stitch
RS	right side
s2kpo	slip 2 stitches tog, knit 1, pass slipped sts over
skpo	slip 1, k1, psso
sk2po	slip 1, k2tog, psso
sl 1	slip one stitch
sl2tog	slip 2 stitches together
st(s)	stitch(es)
St st	stocking stitch (1 row knit, 1 row purl)
tbl	through back of loop(s)
tog	together
WS	wrong side
yd	yard(s)
yf	yarn forward
yrn	yarn round needle
y2rn	yarn wrapped twice round needle
[ ]/*	repeat instructions within square brackets or between asterisks

yarn information

Rowan yarns

The yarns used in this book are all Rowan yarns. Their specifications are given here. If you use a substitute yarn, take care to match the required tension by doing a test swatch of the chosen substitution and changing needle size as necessary.

Cotton Glacé

A 100 per cent cotton yarn; 50g (115m/125yd) per ball. Recommended tension: 23 sts and 32 rows to 10cm/4in in St st using 3.25-3.75mm (US size 3–5) knitting needles.

Felted Tweed DK

A wool-alpaca-viscose mix (50 per cent merino wool, 25 per cent alpaca wool, 25 per cent viscose); 50g (approx 175m/191yd) per ball. Recommended tension: 22–24 sts and 30–32 rows to 10cm/4in in St st using 3.5–4mm (US size 5–6) knitting needles.

Rowan Fine Tweed

A 100 per cent pure wool; 25g (approx 98m/90yd) per ball. Recommended tension: 26½ sts and 38 rows to 10cm/4in in St st using 3.25mm (US size 3) knitting needles.

Siena 4 Ply

A 100 per cent mercerized cotton yarn; 50g (140m/153yd) per ball. Recommended tension: 28 sts and 38 rows to 10cm/4in in St st using 2.75-3mm (US size 2/3) knitting needles.

Wool Cotton

A wool/cotton blend yarn (50 per cent merino wool/50 per cent cotton); 50g (113m/123yd) per ball. Recommended tension: 22-24sts and 30-32 rows to 10cm/4in in St st using 3.75-4mm (US size 5-6) knitting needles.

Wool Cotton 4 Ply

A wool/cotton blend yarn (50 per cent merino wool/50 per cent cotton); 50g (180m/197yd) per ball. Recommended tension: 28 sts and 36 rows to 10cm/4in in St st using 3.25mm (US size 2) knitting needles.

stockists

U.K.
Rowan, Green Lane Mill, Holmfirth,
West Yorkshire HD9 2DX
www.knitrowan.com

U.S.A.
Westminster Fibers Inc,
8 Shelter Drive, Greer
South Carolina 29650
www.westminsterfibers.com

AUSTRALIA
Australian Country Spinners Pty Ltd,
Melbourne, Victoria 3004
Email: tkohut@auspinners.com.au

AUSTRIA
Coats Harlander Ges GmbH
1210 Vienna
www.coatscrafts.at

BELGIUM
See Germany

BULGARIA
Coats Bulgaria
BG-1784 Sofia
www.coastsbulgaria.bg

CANADA
Westminster Fibers Inc,
Vaughan, Ontario L4H 3M8
www.westminsterfibers.coom

CHINA
Coats Shanghai Ltd, Shanghai
Email: victor.li@coats.com

CYPRUS
See Bulgaria

DENMARK
Coats Expotex AB, Dalsjöfors
Email: info.dk@coats.com

FINLAND
Coats Opti Crafts Oy, Kerava 04200
wwwcoatscrafts.fi

FRANCE
www.coatscrafts.fr

GERMANY
Coats GmbH, Kenzingen 79341
www.coatsgmbh.de

GREECE
See Bulgaria

HONG KONG
East Unity Company Ltd, Chai Wan
Email: eastunityco@yahoo.com.hk

ICELAND
Rowan At Storkurinn, Reykjavik 101
www.storkurinn.is

ITALY
Coats Cucirini srl, Milan 20126
www.coatscucirini.com

KOREA
Coats Korea Co. Lt, Seoul 137-060
www.coatskorea.co.kr

LEBANON
y.knot, Saifi Village, Beirut
Email: y.knot@cyberia.net.lb

LITHUANIA & RUSSIA
Coats Lietuva UAB, Vilnius 09310
www.coatscrafts.lt

LUXEMBOURG
See Germany

NEW ZEALAND
ACS New Zealand, Christchurch
Tel: 64 3 323 6665

NORWAY
Coats Knappehuset AS, Bergen 5873
Email: kundeservice@coats.com

PORTUGAL
Coats & Clark, Vila Nova de Gaia 4400
Tel: 351 223 770700

SINGAPORE
Golden Dragon Store, Singapore
058357
Email: gdscraft@hotmail.com

SOUTH AFRICA
Arthur Bales Ltd, Johannesburg 2195
Email: arthurb@new.co.za

SPAIN
Coats Fabra, Barcelona 08030
www.coatscrafts.es

SWEDEN
Coats Expotex AB
Email: kundtjanst@coats.com

SWITZERLAND
Coats Stroppel AG,
Untersiggenthal 5417
www.coatscrafts.ch

TAIWAN
Cactus Quality Co Ltd,
Taiwan, R.O.C. 10084
Tel: 00886-2-23656527

THAILAND
Global Wide Trading, Bangkok 10310
Email: global.wide@yahoo.com

For stockists in all other countries
please contact Rowan for details

acknowledgements

Author's acknowledgements

A huge thank you to the following team of people, without whose skills this book would not have been possible: Steven and Susan for their brilliant work on photography, art direction and styling (and to our lovely gang of models); Anne, for her gorgeous page layouts; our fabulous pattern writer, Penny, and her team of fantastic knitters; plus Katie and Marilyn, for their careful editing and checking; Frances for the beautifully knitted swatches; and the entire Rowan team for their continued support.

Finally, special thanks to my partner, Mark, and Billy and Bunny (our adored cats!), and my loving family.

Publisher's acknowledgements

The publishers would like to thank the following individuals for their valuable contribution to this book: Steven Wooster for photography; Anne Wilson for design; Katie Hardwicke for editing; Ed Berry for illustrations; Therese Chynoweth for charts; Penny Hill and her team for pattern writing and knitting; and Marilyn Wilson for pattern checking. Particular thanks to the parents of the babies and children who modelled the knitwear with both brio and aplomb: Albert, Arlo, Jackson, Junia, Lexi, Martha, Noa (who amused herself and us by creating the scarecrow artwork from surplus props on page 78) and Zena. Special thanks, too, to Harriet Carver, India Cummins, Sarah Sinclair, Sarah Tolner and Catherine Tough for allowing us to use their homes as locations (and thanks to Jem Weston for starting the ball rolling on the model hunt).